T0114978

The High Flier
and
Other Stories

Jairus Omuteche (ed)

East African Educational Publishers
Nairobi • Kampala • Dar es Salaam • Kigali • Lusaka • Lilongwe

Published by
East African Educational Publishers Ltd.
Elgeyo Marakwet Close, off Elgeyo Marakwet Road,
Kilimani, Nairobi
P.O. Box 45314, Nairobi - 00100, KENYA
Tel: +254 20 2324760
Mobile: +254 722 205661 / 722 207216 / 733 677716 / 734 652012
Email: eaep@eastafricanpublishers.com
Website: www.eastafricanpublishers.com

East African Publishers Rwanda Ltd.
Tabs Plaza, 2nd Floor, Room No. 12. Kimironko Road,
Opposite Kigali Institute of Education, Kigali
P.O. Box 5151, Kigali, RWANDA
Tel: +250 787 309702 / 722 562101
Email: eap@eastafricanpublishers.com

East African Educational Publishers also has offices or is represented in the
following countries: Uganda, Tanzania, Rwanda, Malawi, Zambia, Botswana and
South Sudan.

First published in 2011
Reprinted 2016

ISBN 978-9966-25-804-5

Printed in India by
Manipal Technologies Limited

Contents

Acknowledgements

East African Educational Publishers (EAEP) wishes to thank Weaver Press of Zimbabwe (and in particular Irene Staunton of Weaver Press), for permission to reprint the following short stories in this anthology: 'Mukoma Amos' by Chiedza Musengezi, 'Homecoming' by Vivienne Ndlovu and 'The High Flier' by Mzana Mthimkhulu. 'Mukoma Amos' and 'Homecoming' were first published in the anthology *Writing Still* by Weaver Press; while 'The High Flier' was published in *Writing Now*, also by Weaver Press. EAEP would also like to thank *Per Contra Issue 9, Winter 2007-2008*, original publishers of 'The Day Independence Came' by Chika Unigwe, for permission to use the story in this anthology. Special thanks go to Ms Chika Unigwe, the author, for facilitating issuance of the rights. In addition, we wish to relay our gratitude to Ayebia Clarke Publishing Limited (and in particular the Managing Director, Becky Nana Ayebia Clarke), for permission to use these two stories, 'Scars of Earth' by Mildred Kiconco Barya and 'Something Old, Something New' by Leila Aboulela, which were first published in the anthology, *African Love Short Stories Anthology* by Ama Ata Aidoo (Ed). By the time of going to press, EAEP had sought but not received communication from rights holders of the following short stories, 'The Road to Raphile' and 'Jumping Monkey Hill'. EAEP has therefore published them for educational purposes, and would be keen to get formal communication from the original publishers in order to acknowledge them. Finally, we wish to thank and acknowledge the following authors, whose short stories are published in different anthologies by EAEP: Ngugi wa Thiong'o, for the story, 'A Mercedes Funeral', published in his anthology, *Secret Lives*; Leteipa ole Sunkuli for the story, 'They Sold My Sister', published in *Tender Memories*, edited by Barrack O. Muluka and Leteipa ole Sunkuli; and Grace Ogot for the story, 'The White Veil', published in her anthology, *Land Without Thunder*.

Introduction

A short story falls under the **prose genre** of literature. The other genres or types of literature are **drama**, **poetry**, **non-fiction** and **oral literature**. Prose has other sub-categories which are the **short story**, the **novella** and the **novel**.

The general principles of studying literature apply to the short story, and enjoyment is still a key element in reading it. To study literature is to become conscious in your reading of how a literary work creates its effects. Literature as fiction is different from other disciplines like History, Geography or Physics. Fiction's basis is imagination and creativity, though a writer may freely draw upon factual information in presenting the story. The 'facts' may be true or not, but the story would be none the worse if they are entirely imaginary. What we expect in fiction is an authentic **sense** of how people act, not an authentic chronicle of how some few people acted at some past time.

A short story is usually shorter in length than a novella or a novel. It is characterised with economy, and though less intense than poetry, a good short story is concise and can be lyrical. A short story writer skilfully renders a **scene** which refers to a vivid or dramatic moment described in enough detail to create a feel of immediacy for the reader. The writer tries to *show* rather than merely *tell* the events of the story.

Unity and Coherence

The finished short story has a sense of *completeness*, giving the reader an impression of what went before, what is happening now and some sense of a future state resulting from the scene witnessed. The finished story may seem spontaneous and natural, but this is because the writer has written it so artfully that there is meaning even in seemingly casual speeches and apparently trivial details. Missing a detail when reading would lead to missing a significant part, which may compromise the apprehension of the total meaning of the story.

Some short stories tell of an *epiphany*. Epiphany refers to some moment of insight, discovery or revelation by which a character's life, or view of life, is altered in some significant way. Some other short stories tell of a character initiated into experience or maturity. Such a story is known as a *story of initiation*.

Some stories are *didactic*. They carry an obvious moral statement. Usually, a didactic tale has a pattern reflecting a moral order – good versus evil or temptation versus response.

Plot

Plot is central in any creative work of fiction. Plot is the pattern of events, actions and situations. Some patterns are simple, but others are complex. Plot is usually carefully organised to create a certain effect or set of effects on the reader. It can create suspense, humour, satisfaction, sadness, excitement, terror or anger.

The organisation of a plot suggests and emphasises the relationships between characters, events and situations, revealing their meaning with the scheme of the whole story.

When a story opens and develops, a *dramatic situation* is revealed. The dramatic situation is usually based on some sort of *conflict*. Conflict is a struggle or clash within the plot between opposing forces. The conflict may be intrapersonal, involving an individual and his or her conscience when faced with some moral choices. Other conflicts may involve clash of wills, desires or powers between a character and other characters, society natural forces or supernatural forces.

A story begins with an *exposition* which is the opening portion that sets the scene, introduces the main characters, tells us what happened before the story opened, and provides any other background information that is necessary for the appreciation of what will follow. This is followed by the ***complication*** stage where the conflict becomes more complicated as the action develops. New sets of challenges may face the main character (*protagonist*) leading to the ***crisis***. Crisis refers to a moment of high tension in the story. ***Turning point*** is a moment following the crisis, when another set of complication is revealed. This leads to the ***Climax*** which is the moment of greatest tension at which the outcome is decided. ***Conclusion***, also called *resolution* or *dénouement* ('the untying of the knot') is the outcome. The point of crisis and climax is where the theme and the main concerns of the story come out in the open. This is true also about life; it is the moment of crisis that is most revealing.

Hence, plot is the development of events arising out of a conflict and the way they are presented. It is the artistic arrangement of the events that create the aesthetic appeal in the story. The writer may decide to arrange the events in a *chronological order* – beginning with the earliest; or might open the story with the last event, then tell what led up to it. Alternatively, the writer may begin in *medias res* ('in the middle of things') – first presenting some exciting or significant moment, then telling what happened earlier.

Various ***narrative techniques*** are used to enhance the *action* of the plot. They include suspense, foreshadowing, flashback or retrospect, internal monologue or stream-of-consciousness and description, among others.

Point of view

The ***narrator*** or the ***narrative voice*** provides the perspective in a story. The narrator of a story is the one from whose perspective the story is told. The narrator can be a *first person* or *third person*. That is, the narrator can be involved in the action of the story, telling his or her own role in the story, and that of the others. This is the first person narrator. On the other hand, the narrator may be a distant observer, sometimes not a character in the story or even sometimes not named. Such a narrator stands at some distance from the action recording what the main characters say, do, think, feel or desire. In this case the narrator is referred to as the third person narrator. Some narrators are endowed with unlimited knowledge (all knowing), but others maybe impartial and aloof limiting themselves to reporting only overheard conversation and describing without comment or opinion the appearance of things.

To identify a story's *point of view* involves identifying the narrator, that is the part the narrator plays in the story and limits of his or her knowledge of the unfolding events.

When reading a story, take note of the perspective of the narrator, values and personality of the narrator, things the narrator knows or doesn't know; changes of narrator or perspective in the course of the story, and authorial intrusions or comments. Take note of certain characters or things apparently endorsed or criticised from the narrative point of view.

The point of view from which a story is written shapes how the reader experiences the tale. The first person narrator may make the reader feel the full impact of the narrator-protagonist's realisations or experiences. Similarly, the third person omniscient narrator (all knowing reporter) may give the reader a sense of authority and shared responsibility in uncovering the unfolding events.

Different writers utilise different points of view in different ways. Grace Ogot in *The White Veil* uses the third person omniscient narrator. This 'knows all' narrator describes the characters' actions and thoughts to the reader. The narrator projects an air of authority due to the distance from where he or she observes the characters and the great knowledge he or she displays about the characters and events. The narrator gives us a glimpse in the minds of the characters and actions of the main and minor characters. The distance helps establish objectivity and can interpret events and characters impartially. On the other hand, Chika Unigwe in *The Day Independence Came* employs the first person narrator; as such the narrator is a participant in the story, telling us something that happened to her. When telling own story from own point of view, one cannot see into the minds of the other characters like her father, mother and others. As a child, the narrator can hardly understand herself even and thus her power of interpretation is limited. Hence the reader has to be interpretatively active when reading such a story, as his or her wisdom is required to fill the gaps. Usually, the first person narratives utilise *irony* such that the narrators describe what they think they see, but the readers have to interpret the descriptions to discover the 'real' meaning.

Character

A character is an imagined person who the writer uses in the story to advance ideas. The characters are the life of literature – they are the objects in a story of our curiosity and fascination, affection and dislike, and admiration and condemnation. If well represented, the readers can identify and sympathise with a character that may become part of how they conceive themselves, imitate and identify with him or her.

The characters exhibit personality traits that we recognise and even identify with. The writer provides the characters with *motivation* that influence the way they act. The motivation and the traits they elicit give the character a life-like complex personality, making them vivid and recognisable. In Mzana Mthimkhulu's *The High Flier*, the characters of Nxumalo and Lawrence are complex with motivations and impulses for their actions ingeniously weaved out in the story. The reader empathises with Nxumalo, but also understands Lawrence's predicament.

Characters may be *flat* or **round** depending on their role in the story. A flat character has one or a few outstanding traits or features. Round characters are portrayed in greater depth and more details are used to represent their traits. Flat characters may not change in the course of the story, hence are said to be *static*. But round characters are mostly *dynamic*, that is they learn and become enlightened, grow and get better or worse. Mostly the round character is the *main character* of the story. A story can have various *minor characters*, some whom may be flat. *Stock* characters are usually flat with only one character trait magnified or even exaggerated throughout the story. This inflating may deny the character credibility and complexity that characterise real-life individuals.

A round character is portrayed in a complex manner; his or her traits may be conflicting or contradictory. This emanates from multiple impulses but form a single identity of the character. The tension between complexity and unity is what makes characters interesting and credible.

Characters are revealed through different techniques such as dialogue, description, stream-of-consciousness, symbolism or allusion. Writers reveal characters by telling the reader about them through description, or through dramatised action and the reader derive their traits through what the characters say or do.

A *protagonist* is a central character in a story, while the *antagonist* is the character or a force who opposes the protagonist. The action and conflict of the story grows out of the personalities of the characters, and the situations they face.

Setting

Setting of a story refers to the time and place where the action takes place. Setting in a story is more than the physical environment of the story. It Is the location, background or underpinning. It can be central in shaping characters and action of the story. It can prompt characters to act, bring them to realisations, or cause them to realise.

Beside the locale, the time of the story – hour, season, month, year, period, epoch or century – can also matter in conveying the meaning and the atmosphere of the story. It can reveal the nature of the society at a particular time, its attitudes, customs and beliefs. The appreciation of the setting will help the reader to understand the characters and how they act, and the whole story.

Setting can be realistic or imaginary.

Theme

Literature is about things we are all concerned about – life and living. A theme of a story is the general idea or insight the story reveals about its subject matter, which concerns some aspect of life and living. Short stories explore themes that revolve around the characters' ideas about love, marriage, aspiration, death, freedom, hope, despair, frustration, power, war, evil, revenge, and so forth. Writers in their works focus on one or more of these issues and how people deal with them, their contradictory feelings about them and the complex moral and social ambiguities and doubts which confront people making the experience of living complex.

In some stories the theme is apparent, and directly stated. In many short stories the theme is not obvious and must be interpreted from the action of the story, characterisation, the setting and other elements.

A good short story may have more than one theme.

Tone and Style

The choice of details by the writer – the description of scenes, setting and characters, and the words used – convey the *attitude* of the narrator and the author by extension. The attitude so conveyed stir a certain *feeling* in the reader, it can be a feeling of pity, sympathy, resentment or repulsion.

Whatever in a story that leads the reader to infer the attitude of the writer is referred to as the **tone**. The tone of the story is like the tone of voice in speech, it can convey amusement, anger, affection, sorrow or contempt. It implies the feelings of the writer expressed by the narrator or characters. Though the feelings of the narrator and the characters may be dissimilar or opposed, as when the narrator regards the feelings of the characters ironically. This helps guide the reader's attitude towards the story's subject matter and the characters.

Style refers to the particular ways a writer uses words that we come to recognise as habitually his or hers. It involves the writer's mode of expression or how he or she handles language in a peculiar manner. It is revealed in the sentence lengths and complexity, and *diction* (choice of words). Some writers prefer simple, unemotional words while others descriptive adjectives and emotionally loaded diction. Some other writers use words in a precise and concise way, while others are extravagant with words.

Words have overtones, consequently their choice and arrangement in a story is important. The overtone of the words contributes to the total meaning and pleasure the story gives the reader. The words used help suggest the intended deeper meaning. As language characterise people and construct events, the words used should fit the actions of the characters of which they tell.

Similarly, some writers prefer long sentences, others short clipped sentences. Another writer may prefer using long elaborate syntax constructing elaborate descriptive passages that immerse the reader in emotional situation of the story.

The writer's tone also evidences the style of the writer. The tone is an important element of the story's total design. Some writer's have ironical attitude towards their material, some emotional involvement, while others exhibit a laid back attitude bereft of involved feelings.

The arrangement of the material or the design of the plot is also unique to a writer, hence part of the style. Some writers again and again like using chronological order of their narratives. Other built a jigsaw full of flashbacks and flash forwards, with elaborate time shifts.

Narrative techniques

Writers rely on various techniques or devices to write their stories, emphasise themes and achieve aesthetic appeal. Some of the most common techniques are discussed here briefly.

Symbol

A symbol is a thing that suggests more than its literal meaning. Symbols are used in literature to convey a special meaning and give more depth. Symbols point, hint, imply or allude to meaning beyond the perceptible object described. Some characters, settings or episodes in stories can also be symbolic. A *symbolic act* is a gesture that has a larger significance than usual. In Adichie's *Jumping Monkey Hill*, several episodes are described carefully to provide symbolic value. The breakfast talk between Ujunwa and Isabel, for example, is not merely small or amusing talk; it signifies historical perceptions based on prejudice that divides the world.

Symbols are usually forceful because they are concrete yet at the same time fully laden, suggesting and alluding to deeper meaning. It is important to avoid far fetched interpretations for not every image or detail is symbolic.

Tale within a tale

This is a technique used by writers when they want to set the background or focus of a story more forcefully, or want to tie several lightly related stories together. In this technique, there is the main story with characters and action unfolding, but within it, other narratives unfold. The outer tale is the *frame story* within which the other narrative(s) unfold. This technique is employed by Chimamanda Adichie in *Jumping Monkey Hill* and Alex la Guma in *Tattoo Marks and Nails*. The minor tales reinforce the main tale's thematic concerns. The frame story in *Jumping Monkey Hill* is the experience of Ujunwa at the resort in South Africa during a writer's workshop. But there are other stories or stories that are unfolding; the stories that Ujunwa and other participants write are equally meaningful and contribute to the totality of the experience we get from reading *Jumping Monkey Hill*. The frame story provides links between the tales of each participant whose story is discussed. The minor stories provide multiple points of view and reinforce the single message of the story.

Imagery

Imagery in literature is achieved when writers use vivid description to create a mental picture or sensation for the reader. To communicate effectively and help the reader feel what the story is about, writers use imagery as a technique. They evoke a sensory experience of sight, movement, smell, taste or hearing. They help in the construction of setting and characters. Figurative language is important in the representation of image. Hence similes, metaphors, and personification help writers to show exactly what they want to put across more imaginatively. After reading la Guma's *Tattoo Marks and Nails*, the readers feel they know and can vividly see, feel, and smell the prison because of the images the writer has used to bring it to life. We can even in our minds hear the characters speak and see their responses to each other long after we have put down the story.

Irony

This is a technique of indicating an intention, attitude or meaning opposite to that which is actually or ostensibly stated, through word, phrase, character or plot development. An ironic work is organised in a way that give full expression to contradictory or complementary impulses, attitudes or feelings. Ngugi's *The Mercedes Funeral* and Unigwe's *The Day Independence Came* are structured around such irony. In other stories, on varying levels, there are ironic elements and incidences to draw attention to incongruity or discordance.

Description and Narration

Description means representation or giving a portrait in words. To describe is to give some detailed account of something, place, person, action or scene. It helps concretise the story's setting, characters, speech, feelings and thoughts, and conflicts. Description complements and enhances other techniques such as imagery, symbolism, irony among others. Description brings the story to live as details so described are usually carefully chosen and arranged to produce aesthetic effect.

Narration is the core of any literary prose work. Narration is closely linked to the narrator or point of view. A narrator describes, gives account or recounts a sequence of events, episodes or action flow in a story which we follow from beginning to end. The narration can be chronological or not, going back and forward in time.

Speech and Dialogue

Speech or dialogue between characters in a story makes it more realistic. Writers intersperse their stories with conversational exchanges between characters. This helps break the monotony of descriptive passages. Dialogue helps bring the characters in a story to life by helping show them or characterise them by what they say and how they say it. In some cases, what is said and what is not said is important to the meaning of the story, hence speech between characters is complemented with *stream-of-consciousness* and *internal monologue* to achieve a complete understanding of the story.

Interpreting Literature

To interpret a work of literature, you start by noting the facts. Such things as the number and names of characters and the name of place of setting if mentioned in the story can not be in dispute. These facts tell us about some of the choices the writer made. But to understand why the writer made these choices and how he worked them into a unified whole, the question of interpretation has to be addressed. Interpretation deals with the artistic vision that underlay the work of literature. They are concerned with issues of themes, pattern, message, meaning, perspective among others.

A Mercedes Funeral

Ngugi wa Thiong'o

If you ever find yourself in Ilmorog, don't fail to visit Ilmorog
Bar & Restaurant: there you're likely to meet somebody you
were once at school with and you can reminisce over old days
and learn news of missing friends and acquaintances. The big
shots of Chiri District frequent the place, especially on Saturday
and Sunday evenings after a game of golf and tennis on the
lawn grounds of the once FOR EUROPEANS ONLY Sonia
Club a few miles away. But for a litre or two of beer they all
drive to the more relaxed low-class parts of Ilmorog. Mark you,
it is not much of a restaurant; don't go there for chickens-in
baskets and steak cooked in wine; it is famous only for charcoal
roasted goat meat and nicely dressed barmaids. And of course,
gossip. You sit in a U-shaped formation of red-cushioned sofa
seats you'll find in public bars all over Kenya. You talk or you
listen. No neutrality of poise and bearing, unless of course you
pretend: there's no privacy, unless of course you hire a separate
room.

It was there one Saturday evening that I sat through an
amusing story. Ever heard of a Mercedes Benz Funeral? The
narrator, one of those dark-suited brothers with a public opinion
just protruding, was talking to a group, presumably his visitors,
but loudly for all to hear. A little tipsy he probably was; but
his voice at times sounded serious and slightly wrought with
emotion. I sipped my frothy beer, I am a city man if you want
to know, I cocked my ears and soon I was able to gather the few
scattered threads; he was talking of someone who had once or
recently worked in a bar.

1

"… not much … not much I must confess," he was saying. "The truth of the matter, gentlemen, is that I too had forgotten him. I would not even have offered to tell you about him except … well … except that his name surfaced into sudden importance in that ridiculous affair – but, gentlemen, you must have read about it … no? Is that so? … Anyway the affair was there all right and it really shook us in Ilmorog. It even got a few inch columns in the national dailies. And that's something, you know, especially with so many bigger scandals competing for attention. Big men fighting it out with fists and wrestling one another to the ground … candidates beaten up by hired thugs … others arrested on nomination day for mysterious reasons and released the day after, again for mysterious reasons. A record year, gentlemen, a record year, that one. With such events competing for attention, why should anyone have taken an interest in a rather silly story of an unknown corpse deciding the outcome of an election in a remote village town? And yet fact number one … not, gentlemen, that I want to theorise … yet the truth is that his death or rather his funeral would never have aroused so much heat had it not come during an election year.

Now, let me see, count rather: there was that seat in parliament: the most Hon. John Joe James ... would you believe it, used to be known as John Karanja but dropped his African name on first being elected ... standard, efficiency and international dignity demanded it of him you know ... anyway he wanted to be returned unopposed. There was also the leadership of the party's branch: the chairman ... wait, his name was Ruoro but he had been the leader of the branch for so long – no meetings, no elections, ran the whole thing himself – that people simply called him the chairman ... he too wanted a fresh, unopposed mandate. There were vacancies in the County Council and in other small bodies, too numerous to mention. But all the previous occupants wanted to be returned with increased majorities, unopposed. Why, when you come to think of it, why kick a few out of jobs they had done for six years and more? Specialists ... experience ... all that and more. And why add to unemployment? Unfortunately there were numerous upstarts who had different ideas and wanted a foot and a hand in running the very same jobs. Dynamism ... fresh blood ... all that and more. Naturally gentlemen, and I am sure this was also true in your area, the job which most thought they could execute with unique skill and efficiency was that of The Hon. MP for Ilmorog. See what I mean? More beer gentlemen? Hey sister ... sister ... these barmaids! ... *baada ya kazi jiburudishe na pombe*.

Well, after the first round of trial runs and feelers through a whispering campaign, the field was left to the incumbent and three challengers. There was the university student ... you know the sort you find these days ... a Lumumba goatee ... weather-beaten American shirts and jeans ... they dress only in foreign clothes ... foreign fashions ... foreign ideas ... you remember our time in Makerere under De Bunsen? Worsted woollen suits, starched white shirts and ties to match ... now that's what I call proper dressing ... anyway, our student challenger claimed to be an intellectual worker and as such could fully understand

3

the aspirations of all workers. There was also an aspiring businessman. An interesting case this one. Had just acquired a loan to build a huge self-service supermarket here in Ilmorog Shopping Centre. It was whispered that he had diverted a bit of that loan into his campaign. He would tell his audience that man was born to make money: if he went to parliament, he would ensure that everybody had a democratic chance to make a little pile. He himself would set an example: a leader must lead. Also in the arena was a Government Chief, or rather ex-Chief, who had resigned his job to enter the race. He claimed that he would make a very good chief in parliament. Sweat and sacrifice, he used to say, were ever his watchwords. As an example of S and S, he had not only given up a very promising career in the civil service to offer himself as a complete servant of the people, but had also sold three of his five grade cows to finance his campaign. His wife protested, of course, but … sister, I asked you for some beer … we all have our weaknesses, eh?

Each challenger denounced the other two accusing them of splitting the votes. If they, the other two that is, were sincere, would they not do the honourable thing, stand down in favour of one opponent? The three were however united in denouncing the sitting member: what had he done for the area? He had only enriched himself and his relatives. They pointed to his business interests, his numerous buildings in the area, and his many shares in even the smallest petrol station in the constituency. From what forgotten corner had he suddenly acquired all that wealth, including a thousand-acre farm, asked the aspiring businessman? Why had he not given others a democratic chance to dip a hand in the common pool? The student demanded: what has he done for we *Wafanyi Kazi*? The ex-Chief accused him of never once visiting his constituency. His election had been a one-way ticket to the city. They all chorused: let the record speak, let the record speak for itself. Funny enough gentlemen, the incumbent replied with the same words – yes, let the record speak – but managed to give them a tone of great

4

achievement. First he pointed out what the government had done ... the roads ... hospitals ... factories ... tourist hotels and resorts ... Hilton, the Intercontinental and all that. Anybody who said the government had done nothing for *Wananchi* was demagogic and indulging in cheap politics. To the charge that he was not a Minister and hence was not in government, he would laugh and flywhisk away such ignorance. From where did the government derive its strength and power? From among whom was the Cabinet chosen? To the charge that he had made it, he answered by accusing the others of raging with envy and congenital idleness ... a national cake on the table ... some people too lazy or too fat to lift a finger and take a piece ... waited to have it put into their mouths and chewed for them, even. To the ex-Chief he said: didn't this would-be-M.P. ... a man without any experience ... didn't he know that the job of an M.P. was to attend Parliament and make good laws that hanged thieves, repatriated vagabonds and prostitutes back to the rural areas? You don't make laws by sitting in your home drinking Chang'aa and playing draughts. For the student he had only scornful laughter: intellectual workers ... he means intellectuals whose one speciality is stoning other people's cars and property! Gentlemen ... there was nothing in the campaign, no issues, no ideas ... just promises. People were bored. They did not know whom to choose although the non-arguments of the aspiring businessman held more sway. You, your bottle is still empty ... you want a change to something stronger? No? ... oh ... oh ... Chang'aa, did you say? Ha! Ha! Ha! ... Chang'aa for power ... Kill-me-Quick ... no, that is never in stock here ... sister, hey sister ... another round ... the same.

You mention Chang'aa. Actually it was Chang'aa, you might say, that saved the campaign. Put it this way. If Wahinya, the other watchman in Ilmorog Bar & Restaurant, had not suddenly died of alcoholic poisoning, our village, our town would never have been mentioned in any daily. Wahinya dead became the most deadly factor in the election. It was during a rather diminished public meeting addressed by the candidates that the student shouted something about 'We Workers'. The others took up the challenge. They too were workers. Everybody, said the incumbent, everybody was a worker except the idle, the crippled, prostitutes and students. A man from the audience stood up. By now people had lost their original awe and curiosity and respect for the candidates. Anyway this man stands up. He was a habitual drunk – and that day he must have broken a can or two. 'Who cares about the poor worker', he asked, imitating in turn the oratorical gestures of each speaker. 'These days the poor die and don't even have a hole in which to be put, leave alone a burial in a decent coffin'. People laughed, applauding. They could well understand this man's concern for he himself, skin and bones only, looked on the verge of the grave. But he stood his ground and mentioned the case of Wahinya. His words had an electric effect.

That night all the candidates singly and secretly went to the wife of the deceased and offered to arrange for Wahinya's funeral.

Now I don't know if this be true in your area, but in our village funerals had become a society affair, our version of cocktail parties. I mean since Independence. Before 1952, you know before the Emergency, the body would be put away in puzzled silence and tears. People, you see, were awed by death. But they confronted it because they loved life. They asked: what's death? because they wanted to know what was life! They came to offer sympathy and solidarity to the living and helped in the burial. A pit. People took turns to dig it in ritual silence. Then the naked body was lowered into the earth. A little soil was first sprinkled over it. The body, the earth, the soil: what was the difference? Then came the Emergency. Guns on every side. Fathers, mothers, children, cattle, donkeys – all killed, and bodies left in the open for vultures and hyenas. Or mass burial. People became cynical about death: they were really indifferent to life. You today: me tomorrow. Why cry my Lord? Why mourn the dead? There was only one cry: for the victory of the struggle. The rest was silence. What do you think, gentlemen? Shall we ever capture that genuine respect for death in an age where money is more important than life? Today what is left? A showbiz. Status. Even poor people will run into debts to have the death of a relative announced on the radio and funeral arrangements advertised in the newspapers. And gossip, gentlemen, the gossip. How many attended the funeral? How much money was collected? What of the coffin? Was the pit cemented? Plastic flowers: plastic tears. And after a year, every year there is an Ad addressed to the dead.

IN LOVING MEMORY. A YEAR HAS PASSED BUT TO US IT IS JUST LIKE TODAY WHEN YOU SUDDENLY DEPARTED FROM YOUR LOVED ONES WITHOUT LETTING THEM KNOW OF YOUR LAST WISH. DEAR, YOU HAVE ALWAYS BEEN A GUIDING STAR, A STAR THAT WILL ALWAYS SHINE, etc, etc.

You see, our man was right. It was a disgrace to die poor: even the Church will not receive the poor in state, though the priest will rush to the death-bed to despatch the wretch quickly on a heaven-bound journey, and claim another victim for Christ. So you see where Wahinya's death, a poor worker's death, comes in!

I don't know how far this is true, but it is said that each candidate would offer the wife money if she would leave all the funeral arrangements and oration in their sole hands ... You say she should have auctioned the rights? Probably ... probably. But those were only rumours. What I do know for a fact, well, a public fact, was that the wife and her husband's body suddenly vanished. Stolen, you say? In a way, yes. It was rumoured that JJJ had had a hand in it. The others called a public meeting to denounce the act. How could anybody steal a dead body? How dare a leader show so little respect for the dead and the feelings of the public? The crowd must also have felt cheated out of a funeral drama. They shouted: produce the body! produce the body! The meeting became so hot and near-riotous that the police had to be called. But even then the tempers could not be cooled. The body! the body! they shouted. JJJ normally the very picture of calmness, wiped his face once or twice. It was the student who saved the day: he suggested setting up a committee not only to investigate the actual disappearance but to go into the whole question of poor men's funerals. All the contestants were elected members of the committee. Well, and a few neutrals. There was a dispute as to who would chair the committee's meetings. The burden fell on the chairman of the branch. Thereafter all the candidates tried to please him. Rumours became even more rife. Gangs of supporters followed the committee and roamed through the villages. And now the miracle of miracles. As suddenly as she had disappeared, Wahinya's wife now surfaced and would not disclose where she had been. Moreover, the body had found its way to the City Mortuary. This started even more rumours. No beer-party was complete without a story relating to the affair. Verbal bulletins on the deliberations of the committee were released daily and became the talking points in all the bars. People, through the chairman, were kept informed of every detail about the funeral arrangements. Overnight, so to speak, Wahinya had, so to speak, risen from the dead to be the most powerful factor in the elections. People whispered: who is this Wahinya? Details of his life were unearthed: numerous people claimed special acquaintance and told alluring stories about him. Dead, he was larger than life. Dead, he was everybody's closest friend.

Me? Yes, gentlemen, me too. I had actually met him on three different occasions: when he was a porter, then as a turn-boy and more recently as a watchman. And I can say this: Wahinya's progress from hope to a drinking despair is the story of our time. But what is the matter, gentlemen? You are not drinking? Sister, hey, sister … see to these gentlemen … well, never mind … as soon as they finish this round … Yes, gentlemen … to drink, to be merry … Life is – but no theories

8

I promised you … no sermons, although I will say this again: Wahinya's rather rapid progress towards the grave is really the story of our troubled times!"

There was a long pause in the small hall. I tried to sip my beer, but half-way I put the glass back on the table. I was not alone. Half-full glasses of stale beer stood untouched all round. Everybody must have been listening to the story. The narrator, a glass of beer in his hand, stared pensively at the ground, and somehow in that subdued atmosphere his public opinion seemed less offensive. He put the glass down and his voice when it came seemed to have been affected by the attentive silence:

"I first came to know him fairly well in the 1960s," he started. "Those, if you remember, were the years when dreams like garden perfume in the wind wafted through the air of our villages. The years, gentlemen, when rumours of *Uhuru* made people's hearts palpitate with fearful joy of what would happen tomorrow: if something should – ? But no – nothing untoward would possibly bar the coming of that day, the opening of the gate. Imagine: to elect our sons spokesmen of black power, after so much blood … so much blood …!

He too, you can guess, used to dream. Beautiful dreams about the future. I imagine that even while sagging under the weight of sacks of sugar, sacks of maize flour, sacks of magadi salt and soda, he would be in a world of his own. Flower fields of green peas and beans. Gay children chasing nectar-seeking bees and butterflies. A world to visit, a world to conquer. Wait till tomorrow, my Lord, till tomorrow. He was tall and frail-looking but strong with clear dark eyes that lit up with hope. And you can imagine that at such times the sack of sugar would feel light on his back, his limbs would acquire renewed strength, he was the giant in the story who could pull mountains by the roots or blow trees into the sky with his rancid breath. Trees, roots, branches and all flew into the sky high, high, no longer trees but feathers carried by the wind. Fly away, bird, little one of the courtyard, and come again to gather millet grains in the sand. He would

9

lay down the sack to watch the bird fly into the unknown and no doubt his dreams would also soar even beyond the present sky, his soul's eye would scan hazier and hazier horizons hiding away knowledge of tomorrow. But from somewhere in the shop a shout from his Indian employer would haul him back to this earth. 'Hurry up with that load, you lazy boy. Money you want, work no! You think money coming from dust or fall from sky? *Fala wewe'*. No doubt Wahinya would sigh. He was after all only a porter in Shukla and Shukla Stores, an object like that very load against which he had been leaning.

Shukla and Shukla: that's where I used to meet him. I was then a student in Siriana Boarding School. A missionary affair it was in those days, I mean the school and its numerous rules and restrictions. For instance, we were never allowed out of the school compound except on Saturday afternoons and even then not beyond a three-mile radius. Chura township, a collection of a dozen Indian-owned shops and a post office, was the only centre within our limits, both physical and financial. With ten cents, fifty cents or a shilling in our pockets, we used to walk there with determination as if on a very important mission. An unhurried stroll around the shops … then a soda, or a few madhvani gummy sweets from Shukla and Shukla … and, our day was over. Well, I used never to have more than two shillings pocket money for a whole term. So I would often go to Chura without a hope of crowning my Saturday afternoon outing with sodas, *mandazis* or madhvanis. A sweet, a soft drink was then a world. You laugh. But do you know how I envied those who strode that world with showy impunity and suggestions of even greater well-being at their homes? As soon as I reached the stores, friends and foes had to be avoided. I lied and I knew they knew I lied when I pretended having important business further on. Still, can you imagine the terror in case I was found out and exposed?

Wahinya must have seen through me. I can't remember how we first met or who first spoke to whom. I remember, though, my initial embarrassment at his ragged clothes and his grimy face. It seemed he might pull me down to his level. What would the other boys think of me? How quickly school could separate people! At home, in order to preserve my school uniform, I wore similarly ragged clothes and often went to bed hungry. From our conversations I soon found that we shared a common background. We came from Ilmorog. We were both without fathers: mine had died of Chang'aa poisoning: his had died whilst fighting in the forest. So we were brought up by mothers who had to scratch the dry earth for a daily can of *unga* and for fees. We attended similar types of primary schools: Karing's Independent. But while mine came under the Colonial District Education Board, his was closed and the building burnt down by the British. All African-run schools were suspected of aiding in the freedom struggle.

Thus blind chance had put Wahinya and me on different paths. And yet with all our shared past, I felt slightly above him, superior. Deep in my stomach was the terror that he might besmirch my standing in school. But occasionally he would slip twenty cents or fifty cents into my hands. For this I was grateful and it of course softened my initial repugnance. So I, the recipient of his hard-earned cents that helped me hide my humiliation of lies and pretence and put me on an equal footing with the other boarders, became the recipient of his dreams, ambitions and plans for the future.

'You are very lucky,' Wahinya would always start, his eyes lit. He would then tell me how he loved school and what positions he had held in the various classes. 'From *Kiai* to Standard 4, I was never below No. 3. Especially English ... aah, nobody could beat me in that ... and in History ... you remember that African king we learnt about? What was his name ... Chaka, and Moshoeshoe ... and how they fought the

British with stones, spears and bare hands ... and Waiyaki, the Laibon, Mwanga, the Nandi struggle against the British army ... ' He would become excited. He would reel off name after name of the early African heroes. But for me now educated at Siriana this was not history. I pitied him really. I wanted to tell him about the true and correct history: the Celts, the Anglo-Saxons, the Danes and Vikings, William the Conqueror, Drake, Hawkins, Wilberforce, Nelson, Napoleon, and all these real heroes of history. But then I thought he would not understand secondary school History and Siriana was reputed to have the best and toughest education. He would not, in any case, let me slip in a word. For he was now back with his heroes gazing at today and tomorrow: 'Do they teach you that kind of history in Siriana? Only it must be harder to understand ... I used to draw sketches of all the battles ... the teacher liked them ... he made me take charge of the blackboard ... you know, duster, chalk and the big ruler in the shape of a T. You know it?' He would question me about Siriana: what subjects, what kind of teachers ... 'Europeans, eh? Do they beat you? Is it difficult learning under white men who speak English through the nose?' Often as he spoke he would be eyeing my jacket and green tie: he would touch the badge with the school motto in Latin and I often had the feeling that he enjoyed Siriana through me. I was the symbol of what he would soon become, especially with the rumoured departure of white men.

And that, gentlemen, was how I would always like to remember Wahinya: a boy who had never lost his dreams for higher education. His eyes would often acquire a distant look, misty even, and he seemed impatient with his present Shukla surroundings and the slow finger of time. 'This work ... only for a time now ... a few more days ... a little bit more money ... aah, school again ... you think I will be able to do it? ... Our teacher ... he was a good one ... used to make us sing songs ... I had a good voice ... you should hear it one day ... he used to tell us: boys don't gaze in wonder at the things the white man has made: pins, guns, bombs, aeroplanes … what one man can do, another one can … what one race can do, another one can, and more … One day … but never mind!' He always cut short the reference to his teacher, his eyes would become even more misty and for a few seconds he would not speak to me. Then as if defying fate itself, he would re-affirm his teacher's maxim: what one man can do, another one can. Newspapers, well, printed words fascinated him. He always carried in his pockets an old edition of *The Prime* and in between one job and the next he would struggle to spell out words and meanings. 'You think one day I'll be able to read this? I want to be able to read it blindfolded, even. Read it through the nose, eh? Now you see me stumbling over all these words. But one day I will read it … easy … like swallowing water … Here tell me the meaning of this word … de … de … deadlo … ck … deadlock … how can a lock die?' I must say I could not help being affected by his enthusiasm and his unbounded faith especially in those days of lean pockets and occasional gunsmoke in the sky.

Gentlemen, you are no longer touching your drinks. What's left to us but to drink? Drinking dulls ones fear and terror and memories … and yet I cannot forget the last time I saw him in Chura. Same kind of Saturday afternoon. He was waiting for me by the railway crossing. I was embarrassed by this and I affected a casual approach and cool words. He was excited. He walked beside me, tried the customary pleasantries, then whipped out something from his pocket. An old edition of *The Prime*. 'See this … see this,' he said opening a page … 'Read it, read it,' he said thrusting the whole thing into my hands. But still he tried to read over my shoulder as we walked towards Shukla and Shukla Stores.

Did you miss the student airlift abroad?

Study abroad while at home.

Opportunities for higher education.

Opportunities for an attractive career.

All through correspondence.
Apply:
Quick Results College,
Bristol,
England.
P.S. We cater for anything from primary to university.

It was the days of those airlifts to America and Europe, you remember. Wahinya was capering around me. He fired many questions at me. But I knew nothing about correspondence schools. I dared not show him my ignorance though. I tried to make disparaging comments about learning through the post. But he was not really interested in my defeatist answers. His dream of higher education would soon be realised. 'I can manage it … I will manage it … *Uhuru* is coming, you see, … *Uhuru* … more and better jobs … more money … might even own part of Shukla and Shukla … for these Indians are going to go, you know … money … but what I want is this thing: I must one day read *The Prime* through the nose …' I left him standing by Shukla and Shukla, peering at *The Prime*, his eyes probably blazing a trail that led to a future with dignity. Nothing, it seemed, would ever break his faith, his hopes, his dreams, and that in a land that had yet to recover from guns, concentration camps and broken homes. I went back to my studies and prepared for the coming exams. Most of us got through and were accepted in Makerere, then the only University College in East Africa … no – not quite true … there was Dar es Salaam … but then it had only started. No more fees. No more rules and restrictions. We wore worsted gaberdines and smoked and danced. We even had pocket money. *Uhuru* also came to our countries. We sang and danced and wept. Tomorrow. *Cha. Cha. Cha. Uhuru. Cha. Cha. Cha.* We streamed into the streets of Kampala. We linked hands and chanted: *Uhuru. Cha. Cha. Cha.* It was a kind of collective madness, I remember, and those women with whom we linked our loins knew it and gave themselves true. The story was the

14

same for each of us. But none of us I am quite sure that night fully realised the full import of what had happened. This we knew in the coming years and perhaps Wahinya had been right. And what years, my Lord! Strange things we heard and seen of those who had finished Makerere were now being trained as District Officers, Labour Officers, Diplomats, Foreign Service – all European jobs. *Uhuru. Cha. Cha. Cha.* Others were now on the boards of Shell, Caltex, Esso and other oil companies. We could hardly wait for our turn. *Uhuru. Cha. Cha. Cha.* Some came for the delayed graduation ceremonies. They came in their dark suits, their cars and red-lipped ladies in heels. They talked of their jobs, of their cars, of their employees; of their mahogany-furnished offices and of course their European and Asian secretaries. So this was true. No longer the rumours, no longer the unbelievable stories. And we were next in the queue.

We now dreamt not of sweets and sodas but the car, which was now our world. We compared names: VW, DKW, Ford Prefects, Peugeots, Flying A's. Mercedes Benzes were then beyond the reach of our imagination. Nevertheless, it all seemed a wonder that we would soon be living in European mansions, eat in European hotels, holiday in European resorts at the coast and play golf. And with such prospects before my eyes, how could I remember Wahinya?

Travelling in a bus to the city one Saturday during my last holidays before graduation, I was dreaming of a world that would soon be mine. With a degree in Economics and Commerce, any job in most firms was within my grasp. Houses … cars … shares … land in the settled area … these whirled through my mind when suddenly I noticed my bus was no longer alone. It was racing with another called *Believe in God No. 1*, at a reckless pace. I held my stomach in both hands, as we would say. The two buses were now running parallel to one another, making oncoming vehicles rush to a sudden stop by the roadside. It seemed my future was being interfered with by this reckless race to death. And the turnboys: they banged the body of the bus, urging their driver to accelerate – has the bus caught tuberculosis? – at the same time jeering and hurling curses at the turnboys of the enemy bus. They would climb to the luggage rack at the top and then swing down, monkey-fashion, to the side. They were playing, toying with death, like the death-riders I once saw in a visiting circus from India. You could touch the high-voltage tension in the bus. At one stage a woman screamed in an orgasm of fear and this seemed to act like a spur on the turnboys and the driver. Suddenly *Believe in God No. 1* managed to pull past and you could now see the dejected look on the turnboys in our bus, while relief was registered on the faces of the passengers. It was then, when I dared to look, that I saw one of the turnboys was none other than Wahinya.

He came into the bus, shaking his head from side to side as if in utter unbelief. He was now even more frail-looking but his face had matured with hard lines all over. I slunk even further into my seat instinctively avoiding contact. But he must have seen me because suddenly his eyes were lit up, he rushed towards me shouting my name for all in the bus to hear. 'My friend, my friend,' he called, clasping my hands in his and sitting beside me, slapped me hard on the shoulders. He was much less reserved than before and despite an attempt to keep the conversation low his voice rose above the others. 'Still at Makerere? You are lucky, eh! But remember our days in Chura? Those Indians ... they never left ... dismissed me just like that ... But it's good our people are rising ... like the owner of these buses ... the other day he was a matatu driver ... now see him, a fleet of ten buses ... In one day he can count over 100,000 shillings ... Not bad, eh? You better finish school soon, man. Educated people like you can get loans. You start a business ... like the owner of these buses ... do you know him? The Member of Parliament for the area ... John Joe James, or JJJ ... To tell you the truth, this is what I want to do ... a little money ... I buy an old Peugeot ... start a matatu ... I tell you no other business can beat transport business for quick money … except buying and renting houses … Driver, more oil,' and suddenly, to my relief I must say, he stood up and rushed along the unpeopled isle. He had spied another bus. The race for passengers would start all over.

I went away slightly sad. What had happened to the boy with hopes for an education abroad while at home? I soon dismissed this sudden jolt at my own dreams, and tried to re-experience that sweetness in the soul at the prospect of eating a tasty meal. But the death-race had dampened my spirits.

Eh? A glass to recover my breath? Welcome, sweet wine … Sweet eloquence … but what's the matter, gentlemen? Drink also … I say a good drink, in a way, is the blood of life.

You should have seen us a week after graduation. We drank ourselves silly. Gates of heaven were now open, because we had the key … the key … open sesame into the world. Mark you it was not as rosy as it had seemed once we started working. I worked with a commercial firm and all the important ranks were filled with whites … experts, you know … and one stayed for so long in training, it tried one's patience … especially four years after independence … Is it still the same? In a way yes … experts who are technically under you and still are paid more … and make real decisions … still I can't say I have been disappointed … If you work hard you can get somewhere … and with government and bank loans … the other day I got myself a little shamba … a thousand acres … a few hundred cows … and with a European manager … the 'garden' is doing all right. And that's how I get a few cents to drink … now and then … my favourite bar has always been this one … gives me a sense of homecoming … and I can observe things you know … homeboy … after all man has ambitions.

… And occasionally they employ beautiful juicy barmaids … man must live … mustn't he? There was one here … huge behind … Mercedes they used to call her … I prefer them big … anyway one day I wanted her so bad. I winked at the

17

ILMOROG BAR

watchman. I bent down to scribble a note on the back of the bill: would she be free tonight? Then I raised my head. The watchman stood in front of me. He had on a huge *kabuti*, with a *kofia* and a *bakora*-club clutched firmly in his hands. This was a new one I thought. Then our eyes met. Lo! It was Wahinya.

He hesitated that one second. A momentary indecision. 'Wahinya?' It was I who called out, automatically stretching my hand. He took my hand and replied rather formally, 'Yes, Sir.' But I did detect the suggestion of an ironic smile at the edges of his mouth. 'Don't you remember me?' 'I do.' But there was no recognition in his voice or in his manner. 'What did you want?' he asked, politely. My heart fell. I was now embarrassed. 'Have a drink on me?' 'I will have the bill sent to you. But if you don't mind, we are not allowed to drink while customers are in, so I will take it later.' And he went back to his post. I had not the courage to give him the note. I went home, driving my Mercedes 220S furiously through the dark. What could I do for the man? What had happened to his dreams? … broken and there was not the slightest sparkle in his eyes. And yet the next weekend I was back there. That barmaid! But whom could I send? I again called out for the watchman. I argued; he was after all employed for little services like that. And he was taking messages for others, wasn't he? I gave him the note and nodded in the direction of the fat barmaid. He smiled, no light in his eyes, with that mechanical studied understanding of his job and what was required of him. He came back with a note: YES: Room 14. CASH.' I gave him twenty shillings and well, how could I help it, a tip ... a tip of two shillings ... which he accepted with the same mechanical precision. Wahinya! Reduced to a carrier of secrets between men and women!

Occasionally he would come to work drunk and you could tell this by the feverish look in his eyes. He would talk and even boast of all the women he had had, of the amount of drink he could hold. Then he would crawl with his voice and ask for a few coins to buy a cigarette. I soon came to learn how he lost his job of a turnboy. His bus and another collided while racing for a cargo of passengers. A number of people died including the driver. He himself was severely injured. When he came back from the hospital, there was no job for him. JJJ would not even give him a little compensation ... he would talk on like that as in a delirium. And yet when he had not taken a drop, he was very quiet and very withdrawn into his kofia and *kabuti*. But as weeks and months passed, the sober moments became rarer and rarer. He became a familiar figure in the bar. At times he would drink all his salary in credit so that at the end of the month he was forced to beg for a glass or fifty cents. He had already started on *Kiruru* and Chang'aa. At such moments, he would be full of drunken dreams and impossible schemes. 'Don't worry ... I will die in a Mercedes Benz ... don't laugh ... I will save, go into business, and then buy one . . . easy ... the moment I buy one, I will stop working. I will live and die like Lord Delamare.' People baptised him Wahinya Benji. Often, I wondered if he ever remembered the old days in Chura.

One Saturday night he came and sat beside me. This boldness surprised me because he was very sober. I offered him a drink. He refused. His voice was level, subdued, but a bit of the old sparkle was in his eyes.

'You now see me a wreck. But I often ask myself: could it have been different? With a chance – an education, like yours. You remember our days in Chura? Aah, a long time ago … another world … that correspondence school, do you remember it? Well, I never got the money. And it was harder later saddled with a wife and a child. Mark you, it was a comfort. Aah, but a little money … a little more education … school … our teacher … you remember him? I used to talk to you about him. What for instance he used to tell us? What one man can do, another one can: What one race can do, another one can … Do you think this is true? You have an education: you have got Makerere: you might even go to England to get a degree like the son of Koinange. Tell me this: is that really true? Is it true for us ordinary folk who can't speak a word of English? Put it this way: I am not afraid of hard work; I am not scared of sweating. He used to tell us: after *Uhuru*, we must work hard: Europeans are where they are because they work hard: and what one man can do, another one can. He was a good man, all the same, used to tell us about great Africans. Then one day … one day … you see, we were all in school … and then some white men came, Johnnies, and took him out of our classroom. We climbed the mud walls in fear. A few yards away they roughly pushed him forward and shot him dead.'

Wahinya's drinking became so bad that he was dismissed from his job. And I never really saw him in that ruined state because my duties with the Progress Bank International took me outside the country. But even now as I talk, I feel his presence around me, his boasts, his dreams, his drinking and well, that last encounter."

The narrator swallowed one or two glasses in quick succession. I followed his example. It was as if we all had witnessed a nasty scene and we wanted to drown the memory of it. The narrator after a time tried to break the sombre atmosphere with exaggerated unconcern and cynicism, "You see the twists of fate, gentlemen, Wahinya dead had become prominent, even

JJJ, his former employer was fighting for him." But he could not deceive anybody. He could not quite recapture the original tone of light entertainment. There was after all the Chura episode behind us. Wahinya, whom I had never met but whom I felt I knew, had come back to haunt our drinking peace. Somebody said, "It's a pity he never got his Mercedes Benz – at least a ride."

"You are wrong," said the narrator. "In a way, he got that too. You shake your heads, gentlemen? Give us a drink, sister, give us another one. It was all thanks to the rivalry among the candidates. Although they were all members of the committee charged with burial arrangements, they would not agree to a joint effort. Each you see wanted only his own plan adopted. Each wanted his name mentioned as the sole donor of something. After one or two riotous sessions, the committee finally decided on a broad policy.

Item number 1. Money. It was decided that the amount each would give would be disclosed and announced on the actual day of the funeral.

Item number 2. Transport. JJJ had offered what he described as his wife's shopping basket, a brand-new, light-green Cortina G.T., to carry the body from the City Mortuary, but the others objected. So it was decided that the four would contribute equal amounts towards the hire of a neutral car – a Peugeot family saloon.

Item number 3. The Pit. Again the four would share the expenses of digging and cementing it.

Item number 4. The coffin and the cross. On this they would not agree to a joint contribution. Each wanted to be the sole donor of the coffin and the cross. Mark you, none of them was a known believer. A compromise: they were to contribute to a neutral coffin to transport the body from the mortuary, to the church and to the cemetery. But each would bring his own coffin and cross and the crowd would choose the best. Participatory democracy, you see.

Item number 5. Funeral oration. Five minutes for each candidate before presenting his coffin and the cross.

Item number 6. Day. Even on this, there was quite a haggling. But a Sunday was thought the most appropriate day. That was a week that was, gentlemen. Every night, every bar was full to capacity with people who had come to gather gossip and rumours. Market-days burst with people. In buses there was no other talk; the turnboys had field-days regaling passengers with tales of Wahinya. No longer the merits and demerits of the various candidates issues, in any case there had been none. Now only Wahinya and the funeral.

On the Sunday in question, believers and non-believers, Protestants, Catholics, Muslims and one or two recent converts to Radha Krishnan flocked to Ilmorog Presbyterian Church. For the first time in Ilmorog, all the bars, even those that specialised in illegal Chang'aa, were empty. A ghost town Ilmorog was that one Sunday morning. Additional groups came from villages near and far. Some from very distant places had hired buses and lorries. Even the priest, Reverend Bwana Solomon, who normally would not receive bodies of non-active members into the holy building unless of course they were rich and prominent, this time arrived early in resplendent dark robes laced with silver and gold. A truly memorable service, especially the beautifully trembling voice of Reverend Solomon as he intoned: 'Blessed are the meek and poor for they shall inherit the earth: blessed are those who mourn for they shall be comforted.' After the service, we trooped on foot, in cars, on lorries, in buses to the graveyard where we found even more people seated. Fortunately, loudspeakers had been fixed through the thoughtful kindness of the District Officer so that even those at the far outer edges could clearly hear the speeches and funeral orations. After the prayers, again Reverend Solomon with his beautifully trembling voice, captured many hearts, the amount of money each candidate had donated was announced.

The businessman had given seven hundred and fifty shillings. The farmer had given two hundred and fifty. JJJ had given one thousand. On hearing this the businessman rushed back to the microphone to announce an additional three hundred. A murmur of general approval greeted the businessman's additional gift. Lastly the student. He had given only twenty shillings.

What we all waited for with bated breath was the gift of coffins and crosses. There was a little dispute as to who would open the act. Each wanted to have the last word. Lots were cast. The student, the farmer, the businessman and JJJ followed in that order. The student tugged at his Lumumba goatee. He lashed at wealth and ostentatious living. He talked about workers. Simplicity and hardwork. That should be our national motto. And in keeping with that motto, he had arranged for a simple wooden coffin and wooden cross. After all Jesus had been a carpenter. A few people jeered as the student stepped down.

Then came the farmer. He too believed in simplicity and hardwork. He believed in the soil. As a government chief he had always encouraged *Wananchi* in their patriotic efforts at farming. His was also a simple wooden affair but with a slight variation. He had already hired the services of one of the popular artists who painted murals or mermaids in our bars, to paint a picture of a green cow with udders and teats ripeful with milk. There was amused laughter from the crowd.

What would the businessman bring us? He, in his dark suit with a protruding belly, rose to the occasion and the heightened expectations. People were not to be bothered that a few had never had it so good. What was needed was a democratic chance for all the Wahinyas of this world. A chance to make a little pile so that on dying they might leave their widows and orphans decent shelters. He called out his followers. They unfolded the coffin. It was truly an elaborate affair. It was built in the shape of a Hilton hotel complete with story and glass windows. Whistles

23

of admiration and satisfaction at the new turn in the drama came from the crowd. His followers unfolded the cloth: an immaculate white sheet that elicited more whistling of amused approval. The businessman then stepped down with the air of a sportsman who has broken a long-standing record and set a new one that could not possibly be ever equalled.

Now everyone waited for JJJ His six years in Parliament had made him an accomplished actor. He took his time. His leather briefcase with bulging papers was there. He collected his ivory walking stick and flywhisk. His belly though big was right for his height. He talked about his long service and experience. 'People did not in the old days send an uncircumcised boy to lead a national army,' he said slightly glancing at the opponents … He had always fought for the poor. But he would not bore people with a long talk on such a sad occasion. He did not want to bring politics into what was a human loss. All he wanted was not only to pay his respects to the dead but also to respect the wishes of the dead. Now before Wahinya died, he was often heard to say … but wait! This was the right cue for his followers. The coffin was wrapped in a brilliantly red cloth. Slowly they unfolded it. People in the crowd were now climbing the backs of others in order to see, to catch a glimpse of this thing. Suddenly there was an instinctive gasp from the crowd when at last they saw the coffin raised high. It was not a coffin at all, but really an immaculate model of a black Mercedes Benz 660S complete with doors and glasses and maroon curtains and blinds.

He let the impact made by this revelation run its full course. 'Only the respect for the dead,' he continued as if nothing had happened. 'Before brother Wahinya had died, he had spoken of a wish of dying in a Benz. His last wish: I say let's respect the wishes of the dead.' He raised his flywhisk to greet the expected applause while holding a white handkerchief to his eyes.

But somehow no applause came; not even a murmur of approval. Something had gone wrong, and we all felt it. It was like an elaborate joke that had suddenly misfired. Or as if we had all been witnesses of an indecent act on a public place. The people stood and started moving away as if they did not want to be identified with the indecency. JJJ, his challengers and a few of their hired followers were left standing by the pit, no doubt wondering what had gone wrong. Suddenly JJJ returned to his own car and drove off. The others quickly left. Wahinya was buried by relatives and friends in a simple coffin which; of course, had been blessed by Reverend Solomon.

About the elections, the outcome I mean, there is little to tell. You know that JJJ is still in Parliament. There were the usual rumours of rigging, etc, etc. The student got a hundred votes and returned to school. I believe he graduated, a degree in Commerce, and like me joined a bank. He got a loan, bought houses from non-citizen Indians and he is now a very important landlord in the city. A European-owned estate agency takes care of the houses. The businessman was ruined. He had dug too deep a pit into the loan money. His shop and a three-acre plot were sold in an auction. JJJ bought it and sold it immediately afterwards for a profit. The farmer-chief was also ruined. He had sold his gradecows – all Friesians – in expectation of plenty and as an MP, JJJ saw to it that he never got back his old job of a location chief.

You go to Makueni Chang'aa Bar where Wahinya used to drink in his last days and you'll find the ruined two, now best

25

friends, waiting for anybody who might buy them a can or two or KMK – Kill me Quick. It costs fifty cents only, they'll tell you.

JJJ still rides in a Mercedes Benz – this time 660S – just like mine – and looks at me with, well, suspicion! Four years from now … you never know.

Gentlemen … how about one for the road?"

Study Questions

1. How does the author use setting to illuminate the main themes of the story?
2. Identify three main characters and for each list their character traits. How do you respond to the way the narrator depicts the characters you have identified?
3. Explain the relevance of the title of the story bearing in mind the main themes and characters.
4. Referring to four literary devices employed by the writer, explain their effectiveness.
5. Summarise the development of the conflict of the story in 120 words.

Mukoma Amos

Chiedza Musengezi

Nobody sits under the mango tree in our homestead. Mukoma Amos waits there for me to join him every day after school. He is easy to find, like a snail that leaves a silver trail in its path. There is a crisscross of tracks in the sandy clean-swept yard, his movements since morning. I pick the one that clearly shows his palm prints between the near straight line left behind when he drags his feet along. No, it is not just his feet. He drags along the entire lower half of his body, his thighs, legs and feet. People say my cousin is 'dead or useless from the waist down'. It is true that his thighs and legs are lifeless. They resemble sticks with cotton-wool-soft flesh. They grow lengthwise and do not fill out with live tissue. The fresh tracks lead me behind his mother's kitchen, a brick rondavel. I find him slumped against one of the big stones that support the raised platform on which the granary is built. Beside him is a small heap of stones. Is he preparing for a fight? I move closer and I see his shoulders rise and fall to match his hard, fast breathing. He strangles sobs in his throat. He is angry. His eyes look hurt, his mouth, he is on the verge of tears. I touch his shoulder to calm him. He stiffens, shrugging off my hand. I must leave him alone. But how can I?

"What is the matter?" I ask.

He is unreachable. He does not turn his head to look at me. I drop my bag of books next to him. I walk away towards my mother's house, skirting the pumpkin vine that sprouted on its own accord near the rubbish pit. Unpruned, it has grown into a wild luxuriance and is now refuge to the hens' chicks. They hide in it when a hawk eyes them from the air. I climb the anthill behind the guava tree. From here I can scan the entire village.

It is calm and restful. There is no sign of what has disturbed Mukoma Amos. In the village carpenter's homestead stand the two brick rondavels for his two wives and a two bed-roomed brick house with a galvanised iron roof. I stand on the tips of my toes to see beyond. My eyes follow the worn path that leads to the homestead of the village builder, who has annoyed my mother because he wants my elder sister for a second wife. Only when I turn round to face south, and my eyes sweep past Mbuya VaGudza's falling roofs encircled with the overgrown evergreen hedge, do I see three little figures running towards the village head's homestead. The headman's daughters have hurt Mukoma again. They do it from time to time, stopping by on their way from school to humiliate and prod at him with their song. I climb down the anthill. "I'll strike their stupid heads with these," he says fingering a stone. He mimics their song.

'*Nyoka ya Driver, Nyoka ya Driver.*
Ona muhwezva we Nyoka ya Driver.'

"Calling me a snake. Likening my tracks to a snake path. Am I a snake?"

I do not think he expects an answer. The village headman's daughters are untouchable and they know it. Their father owns the land our parents work. He alone assigns land and only he takes it away. Whenever my mother brews beer for sale or for working the fields, she reserves a pot for him. Mukoma's threats to get at his daughters are not empty. I have seen him settle scores with some of the village children. He lures them with the many toys he makes in his solitude. When they are relaxed he grabs one by the ankle and no amount of wriggling and struggling breaks his powerful grip. I pull out my old reader from my school bag. I hand it to him with a promise to come back and practise reading and writing after lunch. I am in the final year of primary school, Standard 6. I am thirteen. Mukoma is sixteen. He does not go to school. I hope to go to secondary school next year.

A story circulates in the village about why Mukoma Amos is 'dead from the waist down'. It is said that it is on account of his mother's character, a woman of flaming passions and an insatiable love for sex. The older 'respectable' women in the village would nod their heads together disapprovingly. 'And God has punished her. Look at that poor child.' Behind her back, they called her Murazvu the flame. I always thought it was because she was a strong woman with a hot temper, impatient with fools and gossips, and only later did I realise that the nickname suggested different fires.

She is tall, washed and scrubbed, her skin shines with body oil. She wears good-fitting floral cotton dresses that her husband, Babamunini Driver, buys from Power Store where he drives a lorry. She is loud-voiced and talks freely. She does not walk serenely like my mother but leaps out to grab the things she enjoys. Everyone in our family looks up to her to break in the young oxen for the plough. She works in her fields and vegetable garden, and her kitchen is never short of food. It was at one of my mother's beer gatherings that a man took the lid off the secret story. My mother brews regularly to raise money for my school fees. This man, who was drunk and boisterous, came up to Murazvu who was singing away. He accused her of willfully crippling her son. The real reason why Amos is crippled, he said, was that for the time Murazvu breast-fed him, she did not abstain from having sex with her husband. She was impatient for baby Amos to turn two, when she could wean him from the breast. The story ends with Murazvu shouting any insult that came to her lips as she thumped him.

My mother is annoyed that I now know the story. She reproaches me for showing an interest in what she calls 'wrong things'.

"Wangwarisa," she says. She thinks I am getting too clever for my own good.

"What if you know the truth, will it make your cousin rise and walk?"

I regret asking her.

"It is not true. Amos was ill and the hospital could not help. It was too late. He should have had an injection to prevent the illness much earlier. That's all."

I risk another question, since there is no anger in her voice.

"What disease was it?"

"Polio."

Clearly her mind is on her clay, she has no interest in taking more questions. She wants it smooth and soft. She stamps it, stopping now and again to pick out stones and lumps.

I have never heard of the word before. I wonder if he once walked. And if so, how did the disease attack him? Did he wake up one morning to find that his legs had given up on him? Or did the disease set in gradually and painfully until his legs grew thin and soft, losing feeling and movement? The questions have to wait. My mother bites her lower lip in irritation before she sends me off to the cattle pasture to look for dry cowdung pats. She uses them to fire her clay pots. When she makes pots she hates distractions. She wants quiet and time alone in which to concentrate. She has all the ones she has made recently out on the kitchen floor. They all have round 'stomachs', as she calls them, of varying sizes that taper into different necks; short, long, wide, narrow, upright and tilted. The small serving bowls are without necks. She polishes them with the small smooth pebble that she picks in the riverbed. She rolls it with enough pressure in her hand to leave the surface with a high polish that she gets with the aid of her spittle. It makes them watertight and gives them a neat appearance. She places the polished pots outside, with their mouths facing the sun so that they can drink in the gentle heat of the late afternoon before she takes them into the heat of midday sun to dry out completely. Then, they are ready for firing. Her pots sell as well as her beer. Village women cast envious eyes at them whenever they walk into our yard. They prefer her clay pots to the enamel pots from Mr Power's store, which heat up too fast and burn food. And they complain that the tin cans cannot keep the drinking water cool. They place orders for *sadza* pots, relish pots, small serving bowls, water pots, beer pot and storage pots. They pay in cash or in kind. Those without money fill the pot of their choice with the *rapoko* that she uses to brew beer. She is a widow and well-known for making money. My father died when I was a baby and my mother, brother, sisters and I all live under the protective wing of Babamunini Driver.

When I come back from lunch Mukoma Amos is calm. I find him leafing through my old first grade *chikaranga* speller. The first ten pages of the book have a colour picture of a person and a word underneath it. The people stand upright with their legs together. Their faces are expressionless, neither happy nor sad. Only their sex is distinct. A man wears a white shirt and a blue pair of trousers and a pair of shoes. Underneath the picture is the word 'baba'. The woman has a blue headscarf and a stripy dress and below is the word 'mai'. I say each word out loud and Mukoma repeats after me just like we do at school. He repeats after me.

"Baba, mai, vana. (Father, mother, children).

But what about them?" he asks.

"Nothing," I say.

My cousin expects a story. He is disappointed that learning is uninteresting.

He yearns to learn: his eagerness exhausts me sometimes. I tell him that we need to practise writing. I smooth the ground and test the depth of the sand with my forefinger. We need more sand for our letters to show up clearly. I get an old dish and scoop sand from where the pots are scrubbed and washed. I smooth the surface before taking his right forefinger into my hand. It feels like my mother's wet clay. He is ready to be guided. I can turn it whichever way I want it to go. I apply a little pressure near the ball of his finger to make a straight line and the smooth half circle to make 'b'. I do it twice more. I let go his finger for him to try on his own. He makes the straight line with confidence but he hesitates on the half-circle. He places it on the left of the line to make a 'd'. I erase it and ask him to try again. This time he puts it on the upper end of the line to make a 'p'. Differences between 'b', 'p' and 'd' are too subtle for him to distinguish. We practise with concentration but progress is slow. I stop with the promise that we will write his name next time. "How about English?" he asks. I promise to teach him 'My name is Amos. My father's name is Driver' tomorrow.

I leave my mother absorbed in her pots when I ask Amos to come and help me gather dry cowdung pats.

"Is she about to fire her pots?"

He does not sound keen but I look at him with pleading eyes. He agrees to come along but not before he knows where we are going to find them.

"Across the road where we graze cattle."

I point in the direction of the cattle pens where the old fields lie fallow, having been farmed to exhaustion. They are sandy and the grass grows short. Big trees are few and far between but bush begins to grow here and there. The fields have been abandoned to allow the land to heal. I hold Amos up by his feet. They feel cold and limp in my hands. He gets on his strong hands and crawls across the road. We head towards the only treed spot where the *muhacha* trees grow closely to form an unbroken canopy at the top. Here the ground is littered with cowdung pats in various stages of dryness. Cattle shield themselves from the afternoon heat in the shade. They chew cud with their heads up and eyes closed, occasionally swishing their tails or twitching a muscle to shudder off flies. We skirt the fresh green and wet cowdung and look for the pats that are baked rock-dry and lift easily from the ground. We gather the pats into small heaps until we have enough to fire the pots. We leave them for collection later with my mother. I ask him about the polio, the disease that my mother said attacked him. He has never heard of the word. His parents do not discuss his condition with him.

In the quiet early morning the ring of the school bell travels across the land to reach the villages in the neighbourhood. The bell is an old ploughshare suspended from the branch of a tree that grows on the top of an anthill, the only rise in the schoolyard. Every morning around five o'clock, from Monday to Friday, a young man strikes the gong with a piece of heavy metal, quickly and repeatedly. The sound reverberates throughout our land. When I hear it, it is time to get up, wash and go to school. If I pull my blanket over my head and lie under it for longer, I will be late for school. I risk being struck on the knuckles or fingertips with a wooden stick ten to twenty times. I detest it, so I am rarely late for school. I like my teacher. Every one of us in our class does. He found his way to our hearts through his missing teeth. His toothless front gums make him like a five-year-old, harmless and vulnerable. The class shows that it feels protective towards him by not causing any trouble. When he talks there is a thsss, thsss sound in each word: booksthsss, cupsthsss, eyesthsss. We understand him without difficulty. We subtract the thss from his word endings and we end up with normal speech.

For our English lesson he gives the topic, 'My Favourite Relation'. He explains the words before we start. "Favouritethss meansthss thathss youthss likethss somethingthss verythss muchthss. Whathss isthss yourthss favouritethss foodthss?"

His question turns the classroom into a forest of hands. Nobody is without a favourite food. They range from rice and chicken to wild fruit: *matohwe* and *mazhanje*. The word is well understood. Next, he explains relation which means your brother, sister, aunt, uncle, all the people you have kinship with. He asks the class to give more examples. We give grandmother, grandfather, niece, and nephew. He raises his left hand and brings the forefinger of his right hand to his lips stemming the flow of our examples.

"Allthss rightthss!" He says with a clap of the hands.

He instructs us to take out our English composition exercise books, choose a favourite relation and write. He reminds us to explain why we like the relation we choose.

I write about my cousin, Mukoma Amos. Words flow through my pen on to paper effortlessly. I know my cousin well, my playmate and trusted friend. I describe how he looks and how excited we got when we discovered that he could flex his big toe. We expected the feeble movement in his big toes to get stronger and spread through his lower body until his legs could stand. I tell how when we are totally and completely alone I sometimes hold down his feet and encourage him to get up. With his strong palms firmly planted on the ground he heaves his body only to slump back as he fails to transfer the weight to his feet. I do not leave out how clever he is with his hands. He makes toys with bits of old wire and the fruit of the sausage tree: a span of oxen pulling a plough, a lorry like the one his father drives. I end my composition with how we practise reading and writing and how much my cousin longs to come to school with me if only he could walk. When the teacher gives back my book the next day there is no mark. An unusual comment at the bottom of my work reads, 'See me'. My heart hammers against my chest. I do not know what I did wrong. I expect the worst, the wooden stick on my knuckles or an afternoon of weeding in the teacher's field. I wipe my sweaty palms against my uniformed thighs as I wait to be summoned.

'Sofiathss!'

He calls out my name but not in a cold warning voice. I kneel before the teacher with my book in hand. He asks if the story is true. I nod. He says my cousin may be able to get some help at this address and he writes it down: 'Jairos Jiri, Nguboyenja Township, Bulawayo.'

As soon as I get home I share the news with Amos who does not show any excitement.

"Do you think my father will like it?"

He has doubts but I trust Babamunini Driver. I keep the piece of paper in the safest place I can find, between the covers of my arithmetic book. When Babamunini arrives on Friday I give it to him. He promises to find out. I cannot tell from the tone of his voice or the expression on his face if he will follow it through.

When he arrives the following week he is driving Mr Power's lorry with his bicycle in the back. Amos has been admitted to the Jairos Jiri School for the disabled. There is a flurry of activity. My uncle cleans the lorry and arranges pillows on the passenger seat to try out sitting positions. When he is satisfied with the arrangement he rolls himself a cigarette. He coughs and blows out a cloud of smoke. He clears his throat and flicks out his tongue to throw out a ball of phlegm. He holds the cigarette between his lips. He unbuttons his overalls heading towards the bath shelter where he takes his bath sitting in the big iron metal basin of warm water. We hear liquid sounds from within: sloshes and splashes, like a big fish in a small pond. Amos's clothes flap on the washing line. Murazvu feels them with the back and then the front of her hand for dryness. Sometimes she pats both her cheeks with the collar of his shirt or the hem of his shorts to feel any lingering moisture in the layered material. She irons them before packing them in a small suitcase.

Afterwards she busies herself with cooking. She is outside her kitchen. With her billowing skirts tucked between her thighs she is bent over a slaughtered chicken, plucking and throwing feathers into a rubbish pit that is close to filling up with fire ashes, dead leaves, left-over *sadza* and broken clay pots. The smell of singeing feathers fills her kitchen as she dips the chicken in and out of flames. This way she gets rid of the tiny feathers that she cannot pick by hand. She cooks rice and chicken, some of which she packs in a bowl so that father and son can eat on the long journey to Bulawayo.

My uncle emerges out of the bath shelter in a change of clothes but not completely dressed. He guides his leather belt through the loops of his navy blue trousers, draws it tightly around his waist and fastens it. He tucks in his shirt-tail and sits down to clean his shoes. With Amos in the passenger seat and Babamunini behind the wheel, the lorry is reversed out of the yard into the road. He shifts the gear stick into first and reverses the engine. Dust swirls all round.

"Roll up the window and keep out the dirt."

Mukoma does as he is told. We exchange glances. A smile lurks on his lips. The lorry recedes into the distance until it becomes a small dot that gradually disappears. It leaves a sad silence behind. Murazvu sighs and tears glisten in her eyes. I glance past her and pretend that I have not seen anything.

"Do you think he'll come back? Walking I mean?"

Her voice is thin and tremulous, she sniffs and snivels. I have never seen her cry. She is a strong woman. I have no answer. I give my homework as an excuse to leave, because I too feel the sting of tears in my eyes. At night I close my eyes and darkness brings me relief. I dream about Amos. He has special shoes on his feet. His legs, now supported with special sticks, hold up his body. He is walking with crutches. I prefer my mind's flights of fancy to the stark reality of day.

Study Questions

1. In note form, list some details used to describe Mukoma Amos.

2. Explain the importance of socio-cultural and physical setting in the story.

3. Briefly describe the narrator and explain his role.

4. What are some of the literary devices that the writer uses to enhance the story's effectiveness?

5. Imagine you are the narrator; use the episodes of the story to write out a four days diary of what happens.

The Road to Rephile

Seam O'Toole

"Hey, Papa Crocs, how long have you been driving trucks?"
"It's been twenty-seven years now."

"Ha, about the time Mandela was in jail."

The greying man seated opposite Moses Skweyiya in the bar smiled, wanly. The truth of the comparison stung. Twenty-seven years.

"I suppose, I've never thought about it that way," he said, speaking in a slow, determined voice. Just like Mandela!

Sam 'Papa Crocs' Ngwenya drained the last of the beer into a clear plastic cup.

"Let's drink to Mandela." Moses raised his cup. "To Mandela!"

"To Mandela." The beer was warm and flat, tasted awful. Sam excused himself for the toilet. His bladder wasn't good with beer; he would probably be up and down the whole night because of it.

He threaded his way past four youths standing around a battered pool table. Despite their buckling legs and drunken shouting, they were alert and looked at Sam with measured hostility. He made sure not to bump anyone. 'Papa Crocs', he hadn't heard the nickname in years. It was only Moses who called him by the stupid name. What was it, twelve years now since Germiston Transport went under?

Sam slipped past the curtain into the toilet. Moses, he thought, peeing, he hadn't expected to bump into him. He was a youth fresh off the farm via Park Station when he first arrived at the company, all wide-eyed and full of jokes. For two years he had been his loader, the stupid nickname invented on one of the lonely routes they had driven together. Papa Crocs, it was harmless enough, Ngwenya meaning 'crocodile', just a bit of respectful tomfoolery really. He had always liked the boy.

While washing his hands he looked around the toilet. It was clean enough but like the restaurant it was bare, not what he remembered. He made his way back past the young pool players, saw two girls, not many years older than his daughter, sitting near the bar, their attention fixed on the television propped above it. Things had definitely changed since his last visit five years ago. He still remembered the old Wimpy franchise. All that this Yebo Yes Tavern offered by way of a menu was a messy scribble of words written on the rear of a beer carton. The new toll road must have been bad for Mr Frank.

Driving down the alternative route earlier this afternoon, Sam had looked forward to seeing Mr Frank, the cantankerous proprietor of Frolich Motors. He had always enjoyed the big man's nostalgic recollections of life in Stuttgart and Windhoek, his larger-than-life story of his arrival in South Africa, on the back of a freight train, loaded with little more than a rucksack and youthful ambition. When Rephile was still young, a mouth of milk teeth, he had often told her about 'the strange German man from the north'. He was just one of an ensemble of fantastic characters from the road that he would use to lull his only daughter to sleep. How things had changed. Rephile didn't need bed stories anymore; the TV seemed to tell her all the stories she wanted to know nowadays.

"How's your wife?" Moses asked as Sam seated himself down.

"Fine."

"And your daughter … what's her name?"

"Rephile, she's fine too. She's twelve now."

"Twelve! I didn't realise it's been so long since the company closed."

"May 1993."

"Eish, you have a good memory, Papa Crocs. Some things never change."

"What about you, are you married?"

"Me, never. I don't need to get married."

"Why?"

"I want to live my own life. Anyway, I have a woman in every town. I don't need a wife, not now."

"How old are you now, Moses?"

"I'll be thirty next October."

"You will need a wife soon, then."

"Maybe, but not now. For now I'm not restricted, I'm unlimited."

Sam thought about the meaning of his acquaintance's odd choice of words, the determined sense of confidence with which he spoke them. Unrestricted. Unlimited. He had never spoken like that when he was young. He married Zandi when he was twenty-two, started driving trucks three years after.

"I'm getting another, do you want one?" Moses said, sweeping the two empty beer bottles from the table.

Sam nodded his head in agreement and then immediately regretted it as Moses walked off. The low, insistent thud of the *kwaito* music had given him a headache. He rarely drank beer, just on special occasions, if his chance encounter with an old contact could be described as that. He should go sleep, he thought, looking at the television where the young women were seated. They were nodding their heads in sync with the beat. "I'm old, I don't belong here. This music is strange." He immediately checked himself. "Rephile likes this music too."

Moses returned with two cold beers.

"Which company are you working for now, Papa Crocs?"

"It's a small one in Roodepoort. The pay is not so good but it is nearer Soweto. You know my wife has asked me to make a plan. She says I must get a job where I can knock off in the evenings, and come back home. This was the best I could find."

"And you? How is your company?" He looked at his companion's faded overall. Even with the company patch removed from the pocket, he immediately recognised it. Moses must have taken it with him when he received his retrenchment package.

"Eish, times are tough now. I think it's better that I pack up this job, Papa Crocs, just drink. I don't make any money doing this job. Like now, for example, I'm on a one-way trip to Durban. It's just a piece job. They gave me train fare to come back, third class. It's better if I find my own transport back."

"I'm sorry, I'm only going to Newcastle. If I was going to Durban you could come back with me."

"Thanks, Papa Crocs, you are a good man … just like Mandela." A cheeky smile came across his face. He toasted Sam, repeated the comparison loud enough for the group of youths to stop their game and look up. Sam gulped down a mouthful of beer. The game resumed. Moses stood up.

"I'm going to talk to my new wife over there," he said, nodding his head in the direction of the bar.

Sam watched his former loader stroll across the room. His stride was confident; he knew what he wanted. He stopped next to a woman standing alone at the counter. She was wearing an Orlando Pirates T-shirt that was way too big for her. It looked like a dress. Maybe that was the fashion these days? Sam did not recall seeing her earlier when he walked from the toilet. She didn't seem part of the noisy pageant grouped around the pool table. She must have slipped in while they were talking. Maybe this was his cue to exit. He would leave the rest of his beer for Moses; he had a healthy enough appetite for the stuff. He motioned to get up.

"It's still early, Papa Crocs, where are you going?" Moses had his arm hitched over the shoulder of the woman. He pulled up another chair.

"Meet Neo." Her smile seemed more like a scowl.

What kind of name is that? It sounds like something off the TV, something that one of the gyrating presenters on SABC 1 late at night called themselves. Neo-Dineo? He pushed his beer over to Moses.

"What, no more, Papa Crocs?"

"No, I think I must go sleep soon. I must be in Newcastle early tomorrow morning."

"Hey, you must be getting old … just like Mandela." He managed to beat his compatriot to it this time.

She had hard, sunken eyes, Sam noticed, her scrawny face not totally unattractive. She wore a large scar above her left eye. A cruel night with a drunken man, he imagined.

"So what happened to that truck Mr Rooks promised you at Germiston?"

"The lawyers took that truck. They auctioned it off. You know, sometimes I still see that truck of mine, fleet number 2701. That was my truck. Somebody has a truck in his name that is actually mine. Even now, it makes my heart bitter."

Moses was not really listening. His hand was playfully cupped around one of Neo's breasts.

"And you, what happened to you after the company closed, Moses?"

"I learnt to enjoy *kwasa kwasa*."

"What?"

"*Kwasa kwasa*! Hey, you know nothing, Papa Crocs. It is music, from Zambia."

"I see. So how did you end up working in Zambia?"

Moses laughed. "No, no, I was with a company that did long-haul into Africa."

"Africa." The word had a warm, unfamiliar taste in Sam's mouth as he repeated it. It tasted like cinnamon and mango and chilli all mixed up. He had never been further than Polokwane with his truck.

"So why did things turn out bad for you?"

Neo squirmed and slapped at Moses' hand. He had just pinched her nipple.

"That long-haul company, they were just crooks. They asked me to sign one of those owner-driver contracts when I started. I was very excited. It was a chance to be unlimited for real. But *daai ding is vokol net* rubbish." He spat the words out. "They cheated me, didn't even register that truck in my name. When I came back from a trip to Zimbabwe, they fired me. They said there were too many of us drivers, not enough work. That empowerment story, I'm telling you, it's just words."

Moses drank another mouthful of beer, wiping the back of his hand across his mouth afterwards. He was smiling again. Something about the outburst lingered, though, reminding

Sam of something he had been thinking of earlier in the day. It suddenly asserted itself.

"You know, this government say they want to empower us but who is monitoring it?" The words felt awkward as they came out. He pressed on.

"You know, Moses, I'm not political, I don't like politics whatsoever, but you see, in this transport job of ours, there are pilots: they are well remembered. And then there are train drivers: they are well remembered. There are also captains of ships: they are well remembered. But us truck drivers ..." He lost his train of thought. It was the beer; it always made his thoughts fuzzy, less concentrated.

"Ai, this old man, he is too serious. Go buy some more beer." It was Neo.

Sam looked at her with interest. She had not spoken at all, merely poured beer for Moses whenever his cup was empty. She met his gaze blankly. There was no hostility in it, just an immeasurable rift. He looked at Moses. His eyes were bloodshot, his fingers playfully concerned with teasing at the ripened nipple silhouetted against her football jersey. He had spoken his words into a void. Sam dropped his head miserably.

How had he lost his train of thought like that? It had been so clear in his mind this morning when he was driving. He had been listening to radio personality Tim Modise on 702. Tim was discussing empowerment. His studio guest was a BEE expert. Sometimes, especially when they referred to a certain act of parliament the talk, went over his head but Tim always seemed to steer it back into his reach, making the educated man clarify his comments. It was why he liked Tim, why he had followed the radio journalist from his slot on SA FM to the static-infested medium-wave channel.

Thinking about the radio reminded him of his bed in the back of the truck. It was time to go sleep. This place wasn't for him anymore.

"Tell Moses I say goodbye."

He felt guilty for slipping away while Moses was in the toilet. But his former loader was now his own man, he would have to live by his own choices now, make good of his new inheritance. In any case, they were no longer a team, not anymore.

A riverine mist had settled over the truck stop. Sam struggled through the haze, searching for his truck. He felt disappointed. He had hoped to see Mr Frank, laugh at his inconsequential jokes. Instead, he got caught in a beery conversation with someone he hadn't thought of in years. Getting into the truck, he wondered momentarily about Neo. She was, however, simply a springboard to other, more pressing thoughts. How long would Rephile still be comfortable nestling under the protective wing of her ageing parents? He didn't want the thought answered.

Sam lay down on his bunk bed, looked up at the photos he had stuck above his head with glue. It was not much but it was something, he thought, studying the photograph of his grey-bricked house in Chiawelo. How many times had he looked at this photo of his house on the southwestern beaches of Soweto? Rephile stood in the foreground, smiling, and just over her shoulder the house's number: 2841. It was painted in white freehand next to the front door. He looked at another photo. It was Rephile on her first day of school; he had been in Durban that day. And Zandi, she had a lonely smile. Twenty-seven years of loneliness. Just like Mandela, he joked to himself.

Had he built a similar shrine to his loneliness? Don't all men in prison? He smiled at the thought as he reached for the Sowetan newspaper he had brought with him. Nights were not the same without Jon Qwelane. After the bosses at 702 pulled him off the air, Sam's evenings were not quite the same.

He missed Qwelane's purposely slow and rambling dialogue, the lack of urgency in his voice as he nonchalantly put down annoying callers, especially those from Cape Town. What had happened to Qwelane? Was this de-empowerment?

He turned to the sports section, studied the photograph of the Pirates player. Rephile said she liked this Vilakazi fellow. Rephile. Lately she seemed less and less interested in where he had been and what he had seen. She was becoming like Zandi, distant. Rephile, to think they had waited so long for her.

"Right, we're back. You're listening to the Tim Modise Network on talk radio 702. As you know, today we have a special guest in our studio, former President Nelson Mandela. This is a rare opportunity for you to talk with Madiba. Call us now; the lines are open. Are you ready for the next caller, Mr Mandela?"

"Yes, Tim, I'm ready. You know I've been ready since 1990."

"Great. Okay, I see we have Sam Ngwenya on the line. Hello Sam, you're live on air. What is your question for Mr Mandela?"

"Yes … hello, Tim, this is Sam. How are you, Tim?" "I'm fine, Sam, what is it you want to ask Mr Mandela?" "Tata Mandela, this is Sam. I am very excited to be speaking with you."

"Thank you, Sam."

"Okay, Sam, so what's your question? Remember, we have lots of callers waiting so make it quick and simple, please."

"Sorry, Tim. Tata Mandela, you know I am a truck driver. Sometimes, well often, I am on the road. Recently, I read your book, *Long Walk to Freedom*. In it you say, 'A man is not a man until he has a house of his own.' I agree. But, in fact, I want to ask you about when you were in jail. Did you ever think about your first house in Orlando West during those years?"

"Now you are asking me a question, Sam. I don't know if I can remember that far back."

"Am I right in saying that that was when you were married to your first wife, Evelyn, Mr Mandela?"

"Yes, Tim. I was still married to Evelyn. I had already moved from that house before I was sent to Robben Island, I was living with Winnie. But you know, Sam, I still remember that house, the pictures of Roosevelt, Churchill and Gandhi on my wall … "

Sam sat up, the newspaper falling from his chest. The cabin's light was still on. He didn't recall switching the radio on when he climbed in, he thought, looking at the console where the radio was installed. It was off. Had he been dreaming all that nonsense? His bladder was full.

Climbing from his truck he could barely make out the garage and restaurant in the near distance. It was quiet. Lonely too. He peed a few paces from his truck. Once back inside, he checked the radio again. It was definitely off. Wrapping a blanket around himself, he looked at the photographs again: the house, Zandi, Rephile. The darkness was absolute and silent when he switched the light off.

"Hello, Sam, are you there? Sam?"

"Yes, Tim, I'm here. Sorry, you know this medium-wave station of yours can be funny sometimes, especially if there is lightning. I think it must be storming somewhere; I couldn't hear you or Tata Mandela." "Well, you must be lucky today, Sam. My producer has just told me that our switchboard cut off all the other callers who were waiting. Is there anything else you would like to ask Mr Mandela? But just before you do, Sam, I just want to tell the listeners to call now with their questions for Nelson Mandela; the lines are open. Okay, Sam, go fit it."

"Thank you, Tim. Actually, Tata Mandela, my question to you is a simple one. I want to ask you about your children. You know, Tata, I only have one child, Rephile. Despite your hardships, you have been lucky, Makgatho, Makaziwe,

47

Thembi, Zindziswa, Zenani, so many children. I want to ask you a difficult question … " "Go ahead, Sam, and please make it quick, I can see our lines flashing again here in the studio." "Okay, Tim, I want to ask Tata Mandela: how can a father be a father when he is far away all the time, in prison maybe? Was it not difficult for you to earn the respect of your children?"

It was still dark when he woke. The darkness, however, was retreating. Some drivers had already switched their engines on. He needed to pee again. His mouth was dry too. Climbing from the truck, he thought about his conversation with Mandela. It had seemed so real, the difficult stammering out of his question, the peculiar manner in which the great man had started answering his question. What had he asked again? The clarity of the dream was quickly retreating, leaving him with only suggestive outlines. He passed a truck that looked like the one Moses had described to him last night. Its curtains were still drawn, the windows steamed over with vapour.

Sam greeted a man stooped over the washbasin as he entered the bathroom area. He looked at himself in the mirror, at the company logo he wore on his chest. "I'm old … just like Mandela," he splashed his face, briskly wiping it with a small cloth afterwards. Looking at himself again as he brushed his teeth, he decided he would eat further along the road. There was nothing left for him here.

The vast, open tract of gravel where he had parked his truck was a mess. Discarded mielie cobs, empty nips of brandy, old cellular phone cards, the sun-bleached core of what looked like a mango pip, even cow dung littered the ground. He stepped over a tyre impression pressed into the earth by a truck. It had hardened in the sun, leaving a permanent spoor on the land. He was lucky he hadn't tripped over one of them last night, he thought; they were everywhere.

He saw Neo approaching.

"Good morning," he tried to sound upbeat.

She walked towards him with a defiant look in her eyes. It was as if the early-morning light had rendered him entirely invisible.

"Good morning," he repeated. She stopped, almost smiled.

"Hello, Papa Crocs," her mouth blossomed with a wistful smile. She resumed walking.

The gears of his truck grated as he shifted into second. It was as if his truck, which lurched momentarily, was also waking up. He passed the truck where Moses lay sleeping. No urgency, just a piecemeal job, he had said. Who could blame him? Sam accelerated, swivelling the steering wheel manically to make the wide, arcing turn. He thought he saw Neo smoking on the stoep by the Yebo Yes sign. As he steered the truck out of the yard, he looked into his mirror. All he saw was the outline of someone, vague and fleeting.

He fidgeted with his radio. What was it he had read in Mandela's book, that thing about the challenge that confronts every prisoner? He couldn't remember. In any case, it was too early for such thoughts. Looking at his clock, Sam calculated that he would reach Newcastle early this afternoon: home, though, was still impossibly far off.

Study Questions

1. What is the subject matter of this story? Discuss with illustrations to exemplify.
2. Sam is conscious of changes around him. Identify some of them and discuss how they relate to the main theme of the story.
3. Discuss the use of allusion and dialogue in the story.
4. Discuss the challenges facing Sam and Moses in their profession. Relate their experiences to those of such workers in your own society.

The Day Independence Came

Chika Unigwe

Independence came one frantic Saturday morning. I was six years old, dressed in pink and waving a small green-white-green flag from the balcony of our apartment in New Lay Out. My feet hurt in my too new shoes. I told no one. Not even Mother. Cars drove by blaring their horns non-stop as if they were all going to a wedding party, *beepbeepbeepppppingbeep.* Sometimes the people in cars waved at me and shouted, "Happy Independence Day," and I shouted back even though I knew they could not hear me above the *beepbeepbeepings* of the car horns.

I waved until my right arm hurt and I transferred the flag to my left hand. I knew what the colours of the flag meant. The green was for our rich land and for joy. The white was for peace. Father taught me all that when he bought me the flag. "We are a rich country. And now with Independence coming, we shall be richer still," he had said. Independence was here and I was supposed to be happy. But the truth was that I was not entirely sure how I felt about it. And my feet hurt in my new leather shoes.

It had rained the day before and so the streets shone like an invisible hand had taken the time to scrub them clean. I could hardly bear to look at them; it was like I was looking at a splintered mirror in the sun. If you looked at a mirror in the sun, you went blind. And no doctor could make you see again. It would take a miracle like Jesus rubbing sand and spit in your eyes like He did in the Bible story we were told at Sunday School. And Father said we should not expect Jesus to come down from heaven to perform the miracles He did long ago. That was why we had to be grateful for people like Zik and Awo who fought to bring us Independence. 'If we waited for miracles, we'd never be free.' Independence put a shine on everything. Made everything new. I heard Father say from the sitting room, 've become a new man.'

Everything glittered. Even the hills surrounding Enugu lost their angry stare. They looked clipped and their greenness was fresh, the colour of spinach. I was going to go to the Polo Park to welcome Independence, which was why I was all dressed up.

But Father changed his mind when the stranger came. He said Independence had come to him. And that was much more important. And Mother was in the bedroom. She would not let me in. My left cheek smarted. And my feet hurt in my new shoes. There was nobody to tell.

In the sitting room, the strange woman sat with a smile on her face and Independence in her arms. Father sat beside them asking, "Can I hold him now? See? He has his father's nose. See? He has his father's hands. Let me hold him now. Can I hold him now? Such a spitting image! Can I hold him now? Isn't he wonderful?" He sounded like I had never heard him sound. He sounded like Ije from downstairs asking if she could hold my doll, if she could comb the hair, if she could dress it up. Father begged as if holding the baby was the one thing he wanted to do most in the whole wide world. And when he finally got his wish, he sighed, "Aah Independence!" as if that one word was the weight of a thousand words. Counting to a thousand made my jaws ache and my throat dry. Mother said when I got older, I would be able to count beyond a thousand. I could not imagine any number beyond a thousand. One thousand was already *aguta aguta gbawa*. The uncountable number. Ije could only count to a hundred. And the twins swore they could count to a thousand but they always found an excuse not to do so when Ije and I challenged them. Ije said she was sure they could not even count to a hundred.

For weeks, nothing else had been spoken of but of Independence that was coming. On the streets, highlife music boomed from cars, throwing the word, 'Independence' into ears. Visitors to the house spoke of how things would change with Independence.

"Life would be so much *sweeter*," Agu, Father's friend said, smacking his lips as if *life* was the bowl of *chin-chin* he had just polished off, chewing with his mouth open, the way my mother had said I was never to eat.

"And you, you don't know how lucky you are. To be here to see Independence," another friend pointed at me.

"Independence will kick the whites out," Father said.

"This. We'll own this!" Agu said, his voice loud, his hand flailing, his good foot stomping the ground so that I wondered if he meant that he would own our house, the furniture or the TV at the corner of the living room. But Father did not challenge him. Just said, "Independence" in a drawn out way as if he were relishing the taste of it on his tongue. Then all three men burst into laughter and started clapping each other on the back. Independence made my father laugh. I laughed along too. Father lifted me on to his shoulders and Agu said, "I swear, this one looks very much like you. If she were a boy, she'd be your exact copy. You swallowed this one and spat her out *one time*."

"Yes," Father said. His shoulders sagged, he put me down and sent me off to play, but his voice had lost its laughter, his face had lost its joy.

I went out into the backyard to play *oga* with the twins from next door who always cheated me when we played. I imagined Independence, a burly bullying man who would kick *oyibo* out. But out of where exactly? And why? And who was this man that could make my father laugh? And make him carry me on his shoulders? And turn the days preceding his arrival into one long party.

Three days later, when Mama Boy, the woman who lived in the apartment below ours saw me in my tight braids, she smiled and said I was ready for Independence. I did not know who Independence was, but I was sure that Independence was more important than a chief because my mother took me down to the market to have my hair braided. And Father bought me a new dress that same day. A pink dress with a satin bow. And matching red shoes with white stripes. The dress looked like something out of my mother's magazines. "For Independence," he said. I wanted to try them on immediately, but my mother tied them up in a *Kingsway* plastic bag and stowed the bag at the bottom of the cupboard in the bathroom. "When Independence comes, you can wear them."

Two days before Independence, my father killed two chicken, asked Mother to pluck them and get them ready for Independence. On the day before Independence came, Mother went on all fours and scrubbed the sitting room floor until it gleamed. I asked her why and she said, "We've been waiting for Independence for a very long time." Father bought himself a face cap with the green and white colours of the Nigerian flag. "It's the patriotic thing to do," he said when I asked. "Independence is big." I did not ask what 'patriotic' was but I wanted a cap like my father's. He said face caps were not for girls and brought me a flag. "You can wave that when Independence comes."

I imagined Independence to be bigger than my Uncle Eze. Uncle Eze was so big that when he walked, the earth shook. Mother said he was that big because he ate little children and I was never to go near him. She also said if I told him she told me, he would gobble me up and I would go to expand his waistline. He was so big it was difficult to believe he was Father's brother. He called Father 'Stick' and teased him that he was that skinny because he married a woman who could not cook well. Sometimes Father laughed. Sometimes he said not being able to cook was the least of his wife's faults. I liked

53

it better when he laughed. It eased his voice, made it fly and tickle us all, including Mother. When his voice turned gruff, Mother would turn into herself and try to become invisible. Her body would slouch from her trying to hide inside it. Mostly, she disappeared into the bedroom. And mostly, he followed her in there. He would come out afterwards and leave the house and when Mother eventually came out, her eyes were always red like she had *apollo*, and she would hug me and say, "A daughter is also a child. I'm not God. *Nwa bu nwa*."

On Saturday morning, Mother dressed me up in my pink dress. She put a red ribbon in my hair, looping it between the braids gathered into a basket at the top of my head. She had on a new wrapper with the faces of Zik and Awo patterned on it, and encircling the faces, the date of Independence's arrival: 1 October 1960. Father was not yet ready. He said we had to wait for him. I danced on the spot to stop my toes from hurting. Mother said, "We'll wait for you downstairs. Ezi cannot keep still." We went downstairs to wait for Father. Mama Boy was in front of her door. She was going to welcome Independence too. "I'll wait with you, she said. It's no fun going alone." She teased Mother that she looked like a new wife.

"I feel like one too," Mother said and winked. "Independence is a good thing. I wish it came everyday."

"If it did, you'd no longer be able to walk!" Mama Boy said.

I asked why, but Mother looked at Mama Boy and they both started to laugh a grown-up laughter that firmly locked me out.

Mama Boy said I looked beautiful. I did not tell her that my feet hurt in my new shoes. I wriggled my toes to ease the pain but it did not help. Mother said, "Ezi, stop being so fidgety please." I thought of telling her the truth. Then I thought better not. I did not want her to take my new shoes away from me. A taxi stopped in front of the house. Mother said, "Isn't it too early for guests? It's not even gone ten o'clock yet." Mama Boy said, "And on Independence day *sef!* I hope no one has died. "

"God forbid," Mother said. "This is not the day for such bad news."

The stranger was a woman with huge braids and a bundle in her arms. She looked at a sheet of a paper in her right hand, looked at the address on the house and came out. Slung from her shoulders was a big brown bag. She walked with slow measured steps as if she was marching to a rhythm played out for her. *One -two, one-two, igba nni na ofe. One-two, one-two, igba nni na ofe*. She looked like a photograph: the smile on her face that was directed to no one, the serenity in her eyes, the stiffness in her arms with the rainbow-coloured bundle, all had the same set to them as the photographs displayed in front of *Goodwill Lucky's International Photo Studio; Your Photographer for Every Occasion. One Trial Will Convince You.*

We took a family photograph there once. Goodwill Lucky, sweaty and firm, told Father that we looked like a family that would look good behind the sunset. He told Mother, "Imagine standing at the seaside with the sun setting gloriously behind you. I shall make you look like superstars." Father said he just wanted a picture, he did not want to be a superstar. Goodwill Lucky looked at Father as if he pitied him, pulled out a huge cardboard drawing and sat us on three stools in front of the sea and the setting sun and a little white boy stooping with his feet in the water and his back turned to us. He told us when to smile, how to fold our arms, how to tilt our heads, how to fix our stare. He said when we came back for another photograph, he would place us in *Parees* with the *Eyefil Tawa* beside us. "Many people like that one, but today you looked great in the sunset. When you come back with a son, nothing but the *Tawa* for you." Mother said nothing. Father said, "May your words reach God's ear. Every man deserves a son, no?"

When the woman who looked like a photograph came close to us, Mother smiled at her and Mama Boy smiled at her. Mama Boy asked, "Boy or girl?"

"Boy," the woman said in a voice sweetened with pride. I thought if I cut into her voice, if I took a slice, it would taste like the birthday cake Mother bought for my birthday last month. She bought it from a Filipino woman whose bakery had just opened. It had fruit and cream on top and soft, soft cake underneath. It was the softest, tastiest cake I had ever eaten. It was September and school had just opened. I took a slice for my class teacher and she said she had never eaten any cake as tasty. When she asked if my mother baked it, I said yes.

Mother's eyes looked sad when the woman said it was a boy.

"He's only five days old." She pushed the bundle in front of Mama Boy and Mother.

Mama Boy peered in. "Beautiful baby," she said.

Mother peered in. She put a finger in his fist. "He has quite a good grasp for his age," she said.

The woman lowered the bundle for me to see. The baby looked angry. His face was powdered. His head and ears were covered with a knitted cap. He opened his mouth and yawned. He was toothless, all gums like the oldest man in my village. The man scared me and every time we went to visit him, I would hold on to my mother's hand. I did not like the baby. I looked away.

"What's his name?" Mama Boy asked.

"We call him Independence. But his real name is Sylvanus. Named for his father. I've brought him to see his father. He lives here. Upstairs."

"Sylvanus is my daddy's name," I said.

Mother slapped me hard on my left cheek.

Mama Boy let out a gasp.

Mother ran upstairs screaming my father's name. I ran after her, my palm soothing my hurt.

Behind us, the woman with the baby called Independence walked with the same sure steps. *One-two, one-two, igba nni na ofe. One-two, one-two, igba nni na ofe.*

Independence started to wail.

Study Questions

1. Explain briefly the appropriateness of the title of the story to the content.
2. Briefly comment on the subject matter of the story.
3. Discuss the accomplishment of the point of view the author has chosen to tell the story. Is it appropriate in your view?
4. Compare the representation of men and women characters in the story.
5. Write an essay discussing how suspense and coincidence are used by the author to illuminate various issues in the life of the narrator.

Scars of Earth

Mildred Kiconco Barya

The journey found us. Long after it was over, I returned to the place of first love.

My mother was the first person to hug me when I reached home. She felt my flesh, my bones, my heart.

"You've lost so much weight, dear child!"

"It's been a hectic life, Mama." That's normal justification when you live in the city.

Dad appeared from the farm gate just across the compound, carrying a large cabbage that weighed about 10 kilograms. He was wearing his usual calf-length black boots, being the farmer he's always been. A surge of fondness welled up in me. He held me for over five minutes, until his red cotton shirt was warm and wet with my tears.

"Welcome home," he said. But I know he did not have to say those words, for they were carried on his hands as he smoothed and flattened my back. They were said in the way he hugged me, his eyes searching for the soul in me, his heart bleeding for me.

Mama whistled and sung at the same time. She stroked my dreadlocks like I had not stormed out of the house threatening no return, tired of the country life.

Wind blows in the eucalyptus trees. I stand still in the compound, consciously smelling the honeysuckle that's grown wildly on our fence. I inhale the sweet nectar and stretch out my arms to gather and hold as much sweetness as I can contain. I want to cuddle the earth and holler that this is where I belong.

I want to clasp time in the cold palms of my hands and not look back to wonder where my years have gone.

Mama disappears into the kitchen and shortly returns with a pot of coffee.

"I have mixed all the spices you used to love."

"Yes, I smell the cinnamon, especially."

"We shall sit here, outside."

The sun is setting behind the hills. The sky wraps around herself a beautiful purple hue; it makes me want to weep. In our dreams, that's the colour we had chosen for the wedding clothes.

I hold the coffee cup and it warms my hands. I want it to reach the ice on the outside but it does not, cannot. Mama is across the table, silent. I could sit here forever in the quiet. "Whenever I watch the golden sunset, your face breaks right through," she says.

"You used to threaten me that *Lakelekele*, the green monster, would kidnap me if I did not move into the house."

"You didn't even fear the mosquitoes. You were so loyal to that sunset you had no life indoors."

I fight the desperate urge to cry. Just like me, sunsets were his favourite.

Sanyu, the girl who lost both her parents and ended up staying home, is laying the table for dinner. Dish after dish, she puts food on the tablemats and invites us to eat. Dad has completed his evening tasks, checking the paddocks and making sure all the farm gates are closed. He hangs his long coat on the nail in the dining room and joins us at the table.

"Lord God we thank you for your provisions that never run out, and we thank you for Nama who is with us tonight. Sanctify this food that it may nourish us, in Jesus' name we pray." Dad's prayers were always brief and to the point.

"God has the whole universe crying to him, he doesn't need an essay to answer us," he would say, when we told him, that the reverend would call his requests 'popcorn prayers bursting out so fast'.

"Nama, here's your favourite dodo," he says, giving me the vegetables I've long missed.

"And here, groundnuts in mushroom sauce."

"Here, your roast pumpkin, you used to love that, remember!"

"Oh yeah, thanks." My voice can hardly manage to audibly pass through the maze of food in my mouth.

"And this is smoked beef in simsim paste; there's your chicken breast; the mashed Irish potatoes you liked as a child; here's the eggplant mixed with bitter tomatoes; sliced carrot in tender bean-pods; rice sprinkled with newly-picked peas and cardamoms, and your favourite millet bread …" Dad keeps passing round more of this and more of that.

The feast melts my heart. Then jugs of sweet porridge, sour porridge, fermented pineapple juice, sour milk, hot African tea flavoured with ginger, and every type of tropical fruit to be found in Kigezi. Sanyu has taken care to cut the water melon in triangular shapes, papaya in rectangular blocks, mangoes and avocados in oval shapes, oranges and guavas in crescent shapes, the berries retaining their round shapes … they dance before my eyes, and I pray to the Lord to make me brave so I do not make a mess of myself.

The conversation is punctuated with lightness, laughter and talking spoons. Even when we discuss sad issues that are the village's concern we connect like I haven't been away too long, like I just slept yesterday and woke up today with no estrangement between us. We discuss the sand and bricks business that's a trademark of our village; the neighbour's son who drowned; the couple who are going blind with age; heavy rains that flood our gardens from time to time; the villagers who have died of AIDS … we talk long into the night. When I finally retire to my room, I stretch out on the bed and listen to the once familiar songs of frogs croaking in the swamp nearby.

The cockroaches stir the night with their melodies; the crickets make known their high stereo pitches.

Through my curtain-less window, the night is seductive. I summon the verdant green trees to be my shade. I see the moon peep to greet me with her smile. I smile back. The stars shine brilliantly and I marvel how they are held up there, without falling, while we who walk the earth where we are supposed to be from, are always in a fall.

She walks into my room unannounced. I am watching the sun rise to the sorghum fields in the horizon. She puts her hands flat on my shoulders and works out a soothing massage. Because I cannot laugh or cry, I heave a pregnant sigh of relief. Gently she caresses my neck, my face and my tangled hair.

"You love my locks?"

She ignores the question. Her hands magically snake through the locks and squeeze my scalp. Energy flows back into me through her hands. This woman that is mother is a god. With her restorative touch, my walls come down in total release.

"His name was Selestino," I say. "We did not set out on a trip, yet a few months later we embraced the future and talked wedding plans."

Mama knows how near the surface my buried hurts are. She works her way, from the surface to the deep, slowly moving down my back, circling rings of spine softly but firmly. I close my eyes and relax.

"He was an economist, he loved reading my dark poetry. All is gone and a wound grows festering inch by inch."

The hands touch parts I'd never known to feel the kind of sensation I was getting. The kind of weightlessness that comes with being a leaf floating on a wave. The kind of lightness known only when you're touched by love.

"I remember mostly how he made me feel. With Tino, love was not the fiery passion of a bush in flames, but a calm fire kindled from beneath and brought out in soft whispers."

Her hands remove the ache from my body, heart and mind. "His love was not the loud hammer that shatters rocks, but the gentle falling drop of water that melts the stone."

"Are you still clutching the past like gold nuggets that cannot be put away?" Those are Mama's first words since the confession. I had thought she would chide me for never telling her about the relationship while it was soaring high.

"I have moved on, but I do not forget. Sometimes I call out to him like deep calls to deep. I see him in rays of the sun breaking through dawn to my day."

"You're throwing away the present."

"The past was beautiful."

"Learn to face the future."

"I can only learn to survive the transition, to accept the interval. Years have gone with the locusts. I still seek his brown eyes to look for the soul that gave me wings."

"I feel your pain," Mama speaks from the depth of her kindness.

"I think love and pain have a symbiotic kind of relationship. They are intertwined like twigs in a crown of thorns. You cannot have one without the other. This I never knew." "There are many things we do not know," she calmly responds.

"You and Dad have always loved each other, how do you do it?"

"We have many lifetimes in a lifetime. Like seasons, we do not take any for granted."

So we talk about winter, summer, fall and spring. Each has a beautiful purpose for which it was created. Each sheds a different life on mother earth. Earth does not complain when spring leaves and there's winter. Neither does she grumble when summer ends and fall sets in.

I recall how I groaned within when Tino left me. When he told me he had prayed and God advised him to cancel our relationship. It was God's doing, not Tino's decision per se. He always took cover in spiritualising everything.

"What else did God say in your prayer?" I had the nerve to ask.

"He showed me another woman."

For a whole week I was a bundle of nerves and only a thin sheet of mercy held me from losing myself. Half the time, I was dizzy and suicidal, the other half of the time I was truly mad.

"I am glad you've come home. I am glad you're sharing with me what happened to you." Her hands are now making repeated performances, playing in my locks and running to and from my spine.

That day I chose to become earth. To embrace each season, each love, each friendship in its lifetime. To release each season when it goes without questioning why or when it would happen again. On nights when I look up, the sky is full of a million stars. Clouds and all, I rejoice to be part of that heavenly orbit. On days when it rains, I open up to the softness and touch of rain and drink to my fill. When the sun comes out, I welcome the warmth, the heat. When the wind blows falling leaves over me, I receive them. I have found the joys of being mellow in spite of the scars. I have been earth since talking with Mama.

Study Questions

1. Summarise the plot of the story in 80 words.
2. Discuss the atmosphere and mood of the story. Refer to the details used by the writer to manifest it.
3. Discuss the significance of home and parents as depicted in this story.
4. In an essay, discuss the use of stream-of-consciousness and any other two devices that complement it in the story.

The High Flier

Mzana Mthimkhulu

The labour officer perused the papers on the Nxumalo case once again. He glanced across his file-laden desk and cleared his throat. I sat on his right holding a folder full of correspondence documents. Titus Nxumalo and the workers' representative sat on a bench on the officer's left. Neither of them was armed with any correspondence.

"Well, gentlemen," the officer began in English, "what language are we going to use in this hearing – the Queen's, or our very own?" His intonation betrayed his preference. The words 'the Queen's' were spat out whilst 'our very own' were lovingly rolled on the tongue.

"We prefer our own language," the workers' representative announced proudly, as if to remind us all that true sons of the soil did not soil their tongues with a foreign language. He pulled the lapels of his blue dustcoat for emphasis. Also wearing a dustcoat but not exuding the same confidence, Nxumalo nodded in agreement.

The officer smiled to indicate his support for the two. "Does the management's representative have any objections?" he challenged me.

In what I hoped was a business-like voice, I responded. "Seeing that all the reports and documents are in English, I think it would only be logical if we stuck to the language." Even before I finished speaking, Nxumalo frowned and shook his greying head.

"Why should we be prisoners of a foreign language?" he demanded spreading out his hands. "I made all my verbal reports in Ndebele. It was our graduate friend here who decided

64

to translate them into English." The three roasted me with accusing stares.

For a moment I saw myself through the trio's eyes – a suave twenty-five-year-old fellow black who was bent on dismissing a hard-working fifty-two-year-old family man. The designer suit I was wearing and the fancy cellphone hanging from my imported leather belt did not help. I quickly squashed that train of thought. I had not burnt the midnight oil at the university and embarked on a gruelling graduate training programme in order to waste my sympathy on losers.

"I have no objections to using Ndebele," I lied. "All I was suggesting was consistency." The company lawyer had advised me to appear reasonable.

Although I am fluent in both Ndebele and English, for me the languages represent two different worlds. English is for Science and Technology and for conducting modern business. It can explain exactly how an internal combustion engine works and how the planets orbit the sun. It can record in detail a business transaction. But I find the language cold and aloof. It falls flat on its face when it tries to convey human feelings. For instance, whenever I bid farewell to friends or relatives, I never feel I've expressed myself properly until I make my farewells in my mother tongue. Similarly, when I tell a worker, "The company is terminating your services," I feel no sympathy for the chap. He is just a faceless statistic and I am doing a job. The whole atmosphere changes if I dismiss him in Ndebele. Before my eyes, the faceless statistic grows flesh, eyes and ears and turns into a feeling human being with a wife, children, extended family and friends. Dismissing him becomes too heavy a burden to carry.

My task at the labour office was to present the management's position so convincingly that the officer would have no option but to agree with the company's decision to dismiss Nxumalo. By agreeing to conduct the proceedings in Ndebele, I had lost round one.

"Home boys," the officer said in Ndebele. "I have studied all the reports on this case and I think it would save us a lot of time if I am frank. This is a straightforward case. In the eyes of the law, the company has adequate justification to dismiss Nxumalo."

This did not surprise me. The company lawyer had assured me that the Ministry of Labour would endorse Nxumalo's dismissal. Nxumalo and the workers' representative were shocked by the officer's summation.

"But Nxumalo did not try to steal," the workers' representative protested.

"It was a genuine mistake. Who can genuinely claim never to err? Even the most agile monkey sometimes misses the branch. Why do you expect a worker to be different?"

The officer nodded in sympathy. "I see your point, but remember that so far there is no dispute on the facts leading to Nxumalo's dismissal. For the record, I will go over them. Two Fridays back, Nxumalo was operating a cash register at Hi-Life Supermarket. A security guard stopped a customer who had just been served by Nxumalo and conducted a random check. The guard discovered that Nxumalo had overcharged the customer by almost fifty dollars."

"How many times must I explains this?" Nxumalo wailed. "It was busy and the new notes confused me. The new twenty-dollar note is similar to the old two-dollar note still in circulation. If I meant to steal, how would I have balanced at the end of the day?"

"Nxumalo!" the officer barked. "Get this into your head. The company is not accusing you of theft, but of incompetence. You failed to give the customer the correct change – and that, in the eyes of your managers, is a serious offence."

The officer glanced at his papers before continuing. "Anyway, to go back to our recap of the facts; both the security guard and Nxumalo made reports to the chief cashier on the incident. Last Monday the company conducted an in-house disciplinary hearing, chaired by the Chief Branch Manager, Mrs Decker. At the hearing the records showed that Nxumalo had not been an exemplary worker. Just in the past six months he had collected three written reprimands – two for late coming and the third for wearing a crumpled uniform."

I cringed with guilt at the mention of the reprimands. As the Chief Cashier, I had issued all three reprimands. On late coming, Nxumalo had explained at the time that he had to catch two buses to get to work. The bus service on the first leg was erratic. "If only the company had a housing scheme for workers, I would live in a house at a convenient township," Nxumalo had concluded. Transport problems were also responsible for the crumpled uniform. On the second leg of his journey to work, he had to travel in a packed mini bus. I had listened to Nxumalo's woes and shaken my head in sympathy.

"Don't lose any sleep over it," I assured him. "These reprimands are meaningless paperwork to be taken off the file within six months."

Nxumalo did not look convinced. "Can I talk to the workers committee before signing?" he had asked.

I shook my head. "Why bother with those whingers? Signing the letter does not mean you agree with the contents. It only means you have seen the letter. If you run to the workers' committee, management won't like that. Remember, it's not the workers' committee which employs you."

"You young, educated people know these things," Nxumalo shrugged and signed the reprimands. "We sent you to college so that you come back to help us with such tricky things. It's nice to see our own people holding positions of authority. And you don't scold us the way Mrs Decker used to when she was Chief Cashier."

"Whites are by nature slave drivers," I said.

Now sitting at the labour office, a bewildered Nxumalo looked at me pleading for an explanation. I looked away.

"At the end of the in-house hearing," the labour officer continued his narration of the facts, "Mrs Decker ruled that Nxumalo be dismissed. These are the facts." He paused and looked back to check if anyone disagreed. We all kept quiet.

"Your only hope, Nxumalo, is to ask your employer to forgive you. I see from the records that you have almost thirty years of continuous service with the supermarket. Surely you must have been doing a reasonably good job for them to keep you that long."

Nxumalo's eyes glistened with tears as he turned to look at me. "Help me out of this one, son. Demote me to a toilet cleaner, suspend me with no pay for a month or so, freeze my wages – anything, but please don't throw me out to the vultures. We all know there are no jobs out there. A devastating drought is ravaging our rural homes. I am the only one in our clan with a job and so I am supporting a lot of people. Most of my children are still at school. I need this job. I swear by the spirits of my forefathers, I never meant to steal." With the back of his hand he wiped off the tears running down his wizened cheeks.

One glance at Nxumalo and my heart melted. I was ambitious, not heartless. I sighed, "Well, I will see what can be done. But you all know that I don't make decisions, just recommendations."

For the first time the workers' representative smiled. "It may be just a recommendation, but coming from you, Mrs Decker will agree. She thinks highly of you."

Pleased with the opportunity to put off making a painful decision, the officer also smiled. "I will postpone making a ruling until we hear the outcome of the recommendation. Gentlemen, the hearing is over." He stood up to shake our hands.

Nxumalo continued to plead with me as we waited for the lift to take us to the ground floor. I mumbled that I would do my best.

It was a short walk back to the supermarket. To avoid being pestered further, I took a different route from Nxumalo and the workers' representative. Ten minutes later I was knocking at Mrs Decker's office. Besides being the Chief Branch Manager, Mrs Decker was my mentor. Eighteen months previously, I had joined the Hi-Life chain of supermarkets as a graduate trainee. Under her guidance I had been placed in each of the supermarkets' sections. At three-month intervals, I wrote reports on how I was progressing. I also made suggestions on how the supermarkets could improve their services and make more profits.

"Come in Lawrence, come in," Mrs Decker said, folding the print-out she had been studying. I sat down. "The figures on the print-out are good. Business has never been better." A smug smile brightened her chubby face. "I have exciting news for you. You know I have always said you were a high flier, and now things are happening." She lowered her voice to a conspiratorial tone. "The manager of our Westend Supermarket is leaving at the end of this month and I am recommending to Head Office that you be appointed to that position. You will be the first graduate trainee to land a managerial position after being with the supermarket for less than two years."

Excitement surged through me but I managed to suppress it. "Thank you, Mrs Decker," I said calmly. "It's kind of you to recommend me for such a busy branch. I hope to get the position."

She gave a hearty chuckle. "I know you will. Head Office has confided to me that all that stands between you and the position is a good recommendation. As I said, I am giving it. The perks of the position include an interest-free housing loan and a company car. By the beginning of next month, you should be driving a brand new Hyundai."

"You have been good to me. I don't know how to thank you." I was truly grateful.

"You deserve it," she said, brushing aside my gratitude with the wave of a hand. "Now, how did the hearing at the Ministry of Labour go?"

"There was a bit of a problem," I began.

"Problem?" she frowned. "I thought that was a cut and dry case?"

"On the face of it, it is. But the labour officer saw it differently. He pointed out that since Nxumalo has been with the supermarket for a long time, we ought to give him a second chance."

"Second chance?" she shrieked. "No way! Let the government employ him if they think he is a wonderful worker. Remember the recommendations you made about three months back on cost saving measures?"

"I remember," I said slowly, wondering what the recommendations had to do with Nxumalo.

"Brilliant recommendations. You pointed out that most of our wage bill was gobbled up by the long serving workers. These old-timers enjoyed high wages but had slowed down with age. They are therefore no longer very productive. You rightly recommended that we retrench them at the earliest opportunity. Thanks to computerisation, none of them will be replaced.

With this Nxumalo, we have to dismiss him quickly before he qualifies for a pension. Unlike staff, workers have to serve for thirty years before they are put on pension. I don't need to remind you that as managers you and I are appraised by the profits we make. So, get rid of that profit-gobbling worker. No stories about long service and so forth."

"But Mrs Decker …"

"No buts, Lawrence," Mrs Decker interrupted in a steely voice. "Look here, I was about to send my glowing recommendations on you to Head Office, but I now have second thoughts. What will Head Office think of me if I recommend someone who does not have the heart to dismiss an expensive worker? You leave me with no choice but delay submitting my recommendations on you until this case is over."

"I have no problems about dismissing a worker," I blurted out. "I was merely reporting what the labour officer had said."

"And what did you say to the officer?" Mrs Decker demanded.

"Me? I told him where to get off. I stressed that there was no way we were going to back down on the case. We were prepared to go right up to the Supreme Court if the Ministry did not endorse our position. Those government chaps don't understand that we are not in the charity business. But I sure gave him a mouthful on how we felt."

"Good. Now you go and complete the case."

"Consider the worker dismissed," I assured her, standing up.

As I walked to my office, I imagined myself driving a Hyundai to my new flat in the avenues area. A dejected Nxumalo was waiting for me outside my office.

"Things did not go well," I told him in Ndebele as soon as we sat down. The least I could do was to send the man into wilderness in his mother tongue.

"I spoke up for you, but the racist bitch would not listen. I am sorry homeboy, you have to go. The whole thing pains me but …" I shrugged helplessly and fell back on my high-backed chair looking devastated.

"Don't be hard on yourself," Nxumalo comforted me. "I am sure you tried your best." He was then quiet and stared straight ahead as if lost. Suddenly he looked much older than his fifty-two years.

About a minute later he stood up slowly. "So this is the freedom and independence we fought for!" he murmured to himself before leaving.

Immediately he left I phoned the labour officer and told him that in spite of my well-argued recommendations, Mrs Decker had insisted on dismissal.

"At least you gave it your best shot," the officer said. "I am writing to advise you that the Ministry has endorsed the company's decision to dismiss Nxumalo."

Five minutes later the Nxumalo case was water under the bridge. The excitement of promotion dominated my mind. I punched the cellphone to call my friends. "What's up, girl?" I began in an American accent. "In less than a month, I will be driving a Hyundai."

"You don't say!" my girlfriend exclaimed.

"Girl, you are talking to the top manotsha of the Westend branch!" I gave her the details of my promotion.

I repeated the call to several of my friends. They showered me with 'congratulations'. I leaned back on my seat and smiled. Why not? I had finally arrived to the world of good living and I loved it. Yes, life was good.

Study Questions

1. How does the narrator's voice contribute to the atmosphere and mood of the story?
2. Discuss three main themes that emerge in the story.
3. Identify and discuss any three literary devices the writer employs in the story. Explain their effectiveness.
4. In a summary of about 120 words, compare and contrast the character of Nxumalo and the narrator.

The White Veil

Grace Ogot

"Sorry I am late, Rapudo," she apologised calling him with his nickname that meant 'slim one'. "The children are doing exams and I had such a heap of marking to clear. I did not realise that it was so late." She slipped in beside him as usual. But instead of making room for her and patting her on the back as he usually did, he snapped at her.

"I am sick of listening to excuses about the children and the school. I always come second to your damn school and your children. I have been sitting here since 8 pm. It is now twenty past eight."

The waiter busied himself cleaning the table which did not need cleaning – Owila had only been in the bar for five minutes. He had seen him come in. Why was he lying to the girl he loved? The waiter looked at Owila and then moved to serve two Asians who wanted some beer.

Achola was taken aback. Her being late once in several weeks could not be the only cause of Owila's outburst. There must be something else. Only two days ago she had waited a whole hour for Owila in that very bar, and when he came panting, she had forgiven him with a smile and they had had a wonderful evening.

The waiter moved towards them again. "What would madam like?" he addressed Owila. "Water, please," Achola butted in. Owila did not protest or show interest. The waiter hesitated a little and then moved. He brought a glass of water and put it in front of Achola. They sat in silence for a while. Then Owila spoke without looking at her.

"I am getting tired of being pushed into second place all the time. I think I should give you time to attend to your schoolwork. When you have made up your mind, we can make amends."

The words pierced Achola's heart. For a moment something blocked her throat completely and she could not breathe. She sniffed and the lump subsided as if she had swallowed it in her stomach and her bowels grew warm as if she wanted to go to the toilet. "What are you talking about, being in the second place, Rapudo? I have loved you and cared for you all my life. That you know – I don't have to tell you. If there is something else I swear I'll not take offence. Tell me!" She fumbled for a handkerchief in her bag to mop the flood of tears that was soiling her green blouse. But Owila was not looking at her.

"Anyway, I've come to the conclusion that you are not serious about me. We have known one another for five years now. You say you love me and each time I ask you for a thing that any man would ask from his fiancé you give lame excuses that cannot fill a basket. Other lovers do it, even some of my own friends. Yet I have to crave night after night because I am waiting to marry a virgin." He laughed mockingly.

"But, Rapudo, this is not the place for us to discuss such matters, let us go for a walk and discuss it. Please."

"No, we discuss anything right here," Owila cut in. "Others are busy having a good time, they will not care about us."

"But the waiters will hear us, Rapudo, please!"

"Forget them." Owila threw his hands in the air. "They can listen if they like."

"Rapudo," Achola said wearily, "if that's how you feel, then let's get married. It's you who wanted us to wait but if you've changed your mind now, I am ready too." She eyed Owila sideways as though there was some mistake, for the man sitting next to her was truly Owila but the words and the menacing voice were not his. The lights in the Rendezvous flickered green, blue, yellow and then returned to their normal dimness again.

"You have to be more sensible, Achola." For the first time in many years he now called her by her own name. He had always called her 'Ataye', her nickname. "Marriage is a long term thing; it will need time. I am talking about the immediate situation."

"But you have never spoken to me like that before, Rapudo. What has happened to you so suddenly that you now want us to break our promise? To spoil the wonderful moments we have shared all these years?"

"Well, I don't want to live in the past," Owila snapped. "I have just realised that I have been a big fool. You think you are more holy than Miss Hannington. Yet she spends the night in John's house quite often and she is a regular Sunday School teacher as well as being an ordinary teacher like you. And I bet that she is in John's house now. But you insist that we can only meet in a bar and when you come to the house you insist that you can't …" He did not finish the sentence.

"I think you are being unfair to Miss Hannington, Rapudo. She may be spending the night there but I don't think she would misbehave."

"What do you mean by 'misbehave'?" Owila was angry. "John is a friend of mine. He himself tells me that you and me are just being ridiculous and old fashioned. He takes precautions and they cannot have a baby. I could do the same if you were sensible and willing to change your outmoded ideas."

Achola looked at her man unbelievingly. She had loved him passionately for a very long time. She lived for him and adored him. He had been a symbol of faith and an ideal man in her life, handsome, kind and holy. Now suddenly he spoke a sharp language that she could not understand. She felt helpless.

"But John and Miss Hannington are Europeans," she said, helplessly. "We cannot put our feet in their shoes.

Moreover, their parents are not here. Nobody knows them here, so nobody will talk."

"That is exactly what I was telling you," Owila snapped again. "You are only interested in what people say. You don't care an ounce what I suffer." He was looking away from her. "Anyway, I have stated my case and I am through." He drained his glass and announced that he was sleepy and wanted to go to bed. Moreover the DC was going on safari tomorrow and he would have to relieve the DO 1. "I do most of his routine duties when he acts for the DC."

Achola sipped a little water. Her throat was bone dry. They got up and walked down the stairs in silence. The waiter watched them go. He knew them. He had seen them at the Rendezvous for many nights and he liked them because they were decent. Some silly couples send you for a drink, and when you bring it, you find them sucking each other's mouths. But these two only held hands. Sometimes he would put 'reserved' on their corner table when his instinct told him they would come. Tonight, as they stepped out of the hotel, he knew things were not well with them.

The streets were bright with lights. But Achola somehow felt lost and darkness was everywhere. She stumbled and nearly fell on the step separating the pavement from the main road. Owila stretched his hands and held her, saving her from falling. That was the only time their bodies came into contact and it was so brief. She stretched her hand out for him but he insisted that he must escort her back to the school. They walked on without talking. At the school gate they shook hands and parted.

Achola did not look back. She fumbled for her key and hurried towards her house. She was almost running. She located the keyhole and opened the door, closing it quickly afterwards. She switched on the lights. She ran her eyes round the room as though looking for something. Yes, there it was. She dashed towards it and grabbed it with both hands greedily.

Her feet could not hold her any longer. She crumpled on her bed. She strained her eyes to look at the life-size photograph that had stood at her bedside for a year. Yes, she was not dreaming. They sat side by side, with Owila's hands resting over her shoulder. Owila was a student at Yala Secondary School then, and she was in her final year at Ng'iya Girls School.

They had since taken several other photos, but somehow that one meant everything to her. It was taken the day Owila slipped the ring on her finger to crown the memories for their friendship and to warn other men that she was 'booked'. They were to marry as soon as she finished her Teacher Training Course. That same night after their engagement, when Owila was seeing her to her uncle's home, she had let him, for the first time, run his hands over her abdomen to feel the pimple-like tribal marks that had been incised on her body when she was a small girl.

"I didn't know your Christian parents would let you do this," he had told her.

Achola replied, giggling, "My grandmother took me secretly. She told me that mother was cheating me. All men including Christians liked a warm and appealing wife."

She stood still and let his hands touch the arched marks under her breasts too.

"All these!" he remarked, feeling good. "You must have endured a lot."

"Yes, it was very painful," she told him. "We stood in a row. The first one knelt before an old lady. She pierced the skin of the stomach with a thorn and slashed it off with a blade. She did the operation repeatedly according to our demands. She was a good old lady – she was telling us that the more you have the more love you will get from your husband. So we knelt before her in great pain but still asking for more."

"I am proud of you," he had told her, while his hands lingered on the raised marks. Then he held her very tightly and crushed her to his chest. When she broke loose to go, he had stood there and watched her enter into her uncle's house. From that time their love had deepened. They had lived as one soul though with different bodies. Achola strained to look at the photo again but it was blurred now. A pool of tears had blotted out the two figures she had seen so clearly before. She wiped the photo and put it aside. She removed her dress but slept in her petticoat. She had no strength to do more.

A little sleep did come to her eyes but the naive remark that Owila had maliciously thrown at her, gnawed at her mind; "John and Miss Hannington do it. We could do the same and I can use those things to stop us from having a baby." The words were so painful that she did not want to think of them but they lingered on in her mind. A thought came to her. Maybe she had been a fool and old fashioned as Owila had told her. If that is what Owila wanted, if that is the only thing that could make her keep him, she would give in, perhaps once or twice. She would write to him tomorrow and apologise and offer to make amends. She buried her head under the pillow and slept.

Owila was in the office earlier than usual. He had had a restless night, and now a cracking headache hit him whenever the outgoing landrover doors were slammed shut. He looked at the pile of mail on his table, but his mind was not there. He walked across the room and took the little photo of Achola that stood in a hidden place over the filing cabinet. He looked thoughtfully at it, opened a drawer and put it there. Just then John walked in without knocking. John was a tall fair-haired Englishman. He was the youngest of the European administration in Nyanza and looked after Nyando Division. A bachelor, he lived in Mohamed Road, not far from the radio transmitters. He was good natured, unlike most of his people who were so withdrawn and cold. He was jovial and believed in life while he was young. John was only 26. His parents lived in the city of London and he had lived there all his life until he came to Kenya. He was friendly to Jenny Hannington, a teacher at Saints High School. He had not made up his mind to marry her, but for the time being they were having a good time.

The friendship between John and Owila developed when Owila was appointed DO in charge of the Winam Division. Owila was 25, only a year younger than John. They got on well. John had found the other Europeans at the station old and rigid in their outlook on life. They had warned him not to be too close to Africans or they would never obey him. But the young DO rebelled and chose his own friends.

Owila felt resentful to see John looking so fresh while he was nothing but a packet of misery. Last night when he walked home sadly from seeing Achola at her school, he saw Jenny's car parked at John's door, and his heart ached. Perhaps John had walked in to boast or to tell him in detail what they had done. John never found it embarrassing to talk about sex to Owila – not because he was loose, but because he liked Owila and they were good friends.

"What is the long face for?" John asked at the door.

"Oh, I think old age is creeping up on me," Owila said, evasively. "I shivered all night. I think I have fever coming."

"Ha, ha," John teased him, "nothing to do with old age. You just need a woman to hug all night. That will overhaul your system completely. You have got a beautiful woman but you never invite her home. You are a fool not to have a good time."

Owila forced a feeble laugh and talked about something else to cover up the pain. If only John knew the number of times he had begged Achola to come and spend even part of the night in his house! But she would not agree because people would talk. He had given in to Achola's wishes because he loved her so much. They discussed some business for a while, and John left for *safari*. The examination started punctually at 9.00 o'clock. Achola could not eat any breakfast so she went to Standard Five and wrote all the questions on the blackboard long before the children came. At 9.00 o'clock sharp, she turned over the blackboard and read the questions to the children. It was a religious paper.

The last question read:

(a) Enumerate the 10 commandments.

(b) To whom did God give the 10 commandments?

(c) In which part of the Bible do you find them?

The children settled to their paper and Achola sat on a small table invigilating. Her swollen eyes ached from the bright light. She took a writing pad from her basket. She must write to Rapudo at once. She wrote a short letter telling Owila that she had thought over their talk, that she would consider his request and that she had had a miserable night. But when she re-read the letter her heart was uneasy. The answers listed on the pink paper before her stared at her. She read the answers to the last question. She did not want to. She tried to think of other things. Yet she found herself searching the lines till she found one of the Ten Commandments: 'Do Not Commit Adultery'. She removed her eyes from the pages quickly – but the words haunted her. They were written everywhere she looked. She turned the paper upside down, but the words remained.

The folded letter stood before her. "What did adultery mean?" She racked her brain. Had she not heard the preacher say that it only meant sleeping with your brother's wife? Or was it not? She could not remember if the commandment also referred to sexual intercourse between a boy and a girl. Should she consult the Bible? It was just there before her. But she was too tired to bother. After all the language of the Bible was difficult, the tribal commandments were easier to remember and they were clearer. 'A girl must be a virgin on the day of her marriage. This is the greatest honour she can bestow upon the man she is marrying and upon her parents.' There was nothing to add to this. Achola was the first daughter, her mother was deeply respected – not only among Christians but among other women. Apiyo, the daughter of Ogo, her age sister who had married recently, brought great honour to her mother and her people when a bedsheet was returned to her home wrapped up in a goat skin. Her mother sat near the fireplace and other women powdered her with ashes because she had brought up her daughter well.

Achola took the letter and tore it into little bits and put the bits in her bag. She had made up her mind. It was all very well for Miss Hannington to give. But she was lucky because she was a European. Perhaps her people did not demand the bedsheet to be returned to the grandmother the day after the wedding.

Tears blinded her and she mopped her eyes. The children were busy with the examination. They would not see her. Something told her that Rapudo would come back to her without the high price he was demanding. No, the quarrel could not last. Rapudo knew full well that she would not live without him, she had refused all other men to wait for him while he was at school. Their friendship had lasted many years, and the numerous gifts they had exchanged were a clear indication to the world that they would eventually marry. Both parents knew about the friendship and they had raised no objection. All that was left was for Owila's people to approach her parents and start paying dowry. The children finished their Religious Knowledge paper and Achola went to the common room for a cup of tea.

On the fourth day after the row, a boy walked into Achola's house and handed her a letter in a blue envelope. She took the letter nervously and studied the handwriting for a while. The boy said no reply was needed and walked away. The letter was brief and simply written. There was no reference to the previous quarrel nor did it carry any message of love. It merely stated that Owila was going to a conference in Nairobi for a week and that on his return he would relieve Mr Wasigu the DO, Bondo Division, who was going to England for six months.

Achola read the letter again and again, each time hoping to isolate a single word that might comfort her. She moved restlessly about the house. She thought of many things. At last she sat down and hurriedly scribbled a short letter. It was not like her writing because she weighed each word again and again before putting it down. The letter read: "Rapudo, your letter has reached me. It has only partially lifted the shadow of sorrow that darkens my heart. I say partially because your handwriting has comforted me. But I yearn for the moment when I will see him whom I live for, whose heart lives in mine. Travel safely and return in peace."

She fingered the letter for a while, then she put it in an envelope and sent it to Owila's house through one of the school-boys. "Do not wait for a reply," she told him. Then Achola sat on the verandah till she saw the boy running back to his class.

The busy examination time ceased and Achola had long miserable days and touchy sleepless nights that robbed her of the health and gaiety of youth. She had never known sorrow to this extent. She had been sick, sometimes she had been mistreated by her seniors when she first went to school, but never anything remotely like this. This was a kind of sickness that was eating all her heart away, burying the past and blotting out the future she had so carefully planned. People who saw her walking thought she was alive, yet in her heart Achola knew she was a sick woman, moving in a big town among thousands of people without really seeing them. Yes, if Owila did not write, the sorrow was catching up with her, it would kill her.

One day, she bumped into John and Jenny at the market, "I haven't seen you for months," John greeted happily. "I hear Owila's doing very well in Bondo – he only complains of too much work. Have you been to visit him there yet?"

"Not yet," Achola said automatically. "I hope to visit him soon."

They looked busy and Achola felt happy when they said goodbye, greatly relieved that John had not asked her if Owila wrote at all. This was the first time that she bitterly learnt that Owila was really in Bondo Division. Two months had slipped by with Achola looking in vain for Owila's letter. That night she dreamt that Rapudo had overturned his Land rover, and broken all his ribs. She rushed to the hospital to see him, but he did not recognise her. He was sweating heavily and his drying lips were peeling away and dry blood coloured his white teeth. Achola walked tearfully to the shops to buy him some orange squash. But on her return after barely half an hour, the nurse told her at the doorway that Owila had died. Achola woke up scared in perspiration and tears. She looked at her watch, it was just midnight. She slept no more.

Then the August holiday came and Achola was asked to go for a refresher course at Vihiga Teacher's Training College for nearly one month. At first she told the headmaster that she was not well and wanted to go to her mother in Ugenya, but something told her to go to Vihiga. Hanging around Kisumu without Rapudo was useless. The evenings had become so dull and long she retired early each night only to weep. When she went home to see her mother for a few days before going to Vihiga, she avoided discussing Owila as she had in the past.

Vihiga Teacher's Training College stood high in the rocky hills in Southern Maragoli. It was harvest time and the millet and maize planted in lines covered the entire ridges so that at dusk they looked like soldiers on parade. When the day's work was done, and the essays written, Achola went out climbing the ridges with a group of old schoolmates whom she had not seen for many years. They talked and laughed about their school days long past, and at sunset, they ran back to the College as the land was closing itself to sleep. Achola would stand at the gates of the College inhaling the evening air saturated with smells of roasting maize and the large unshelled local beans.

The change soothed somewhat Achola's yearning for Owila and she would even imagine that Owila had written and that letters were waiting for her at Kisumu. She ate and slept better and the country air slowly nursed her back to health.

When she returned to Kisumu, the school was deserted except for the Opudo family who stayed there permanently during the holidays. Opudo's wife was a copy typist in town and her holidays never coincided with school holidays. Achola walked straight to their house to check if anybody had called to see her and if she had any letters.

"You look well, madam," Mrs Opudo greeted her gaily.

"What were you eating at Vihiga? You've put on weight."

"Maragoli beans and sweet potatoes, and lots of fresh air."

"That's what I need," Mrs Opudo looked at her thin arms. "One needs a change from Kisumu. This hot air is draining all the oil from us leaving our young bodies ridged like old women!"

They laughed as they entered the house to have tea. Mrs Opudo told Achola about the things that had happened at Kisumu since she went away.

"Oh yes, and two women called to see you, and you have several letters here!"

She ran to the bedroom and returned with the mail. Achola took the mail; her heart was beating wildly as she wondered how many letters Owila had written and what they contained. Mrs Opudo was talking to her, but she was not listening. She waded through the letters quickly. There was nothing from Owila. She looked at the envelopes all over again, not expecting a miracle, but to conceal the rushing tears, and to allow her eyes to focus properly. The hope that had lived with her during her course at Vihiga vanished. Three months had gone, a fourth month would start tomorrow, yet she had not heard from him. Achola thanked Mrs Opudo and left.

The church was full when Achola got there on Sunday. She usually sat with the choir, but today she entered unnoticed and sat at the back. She had no heart to sing – she only came to plead with God. He had given Owila to her to be her lover and future husband. Why had he taken him away? Why was he torturing her so? While the preacher preached a long sermon on repentance and the second coming of Christ, Achola was only half listening. When the sermon ended she wanted to slip away quietly before the usual announcements, but she was sitting in a corner, and to wade through the older women would attract attention. So she sat still, looking at the pulpit. Several announcements were made, then coming marriages were read.

"First I publish the Banns of Marriage between Solomon Ouma son of Manas Owira of Riwa Kisumu to Miss Ana Apiyo daughter of Ramogi, Seme. If any of you knows a just cause or impediment why these two persons should not be joined together in holy matrimony, ye have to declare it. This is the second time of asking."

The clergyman eyed the congregation critically, but there was nobody who raised any objection, so he signed the register. Then he raised his voice again. "The second marriage is between Absalom Owila, son of Simeon Omoro, Siala, Nyakach to Miss Felomena Wariwa, daughter of Oyoo of Usigu, Yimbo. If any of you knows a just cause or impediment why these two persons should not be joined together in holy matrimony, ye have to declare it. This is the first time of asking."

Achola looked at the congregation and her eyes were dazed. Did they also hear what she had heard? She steadied herself a little because she could not breathe and could not hear her heart beating. The hymn book she was holding slipped from her sweaty hands and dropped between her feet. She looked at the pulpit, yes, the clergyman was looking at the congregation to see if anybody had any objection to the marriage between Absalom Owila and Felomena Wariwa. His hand was clutching a pen, yes, he was going to sign it. She must get up quickly and shout with all her strength, "He is mine. Owila is mine – Rapudo is mine."

But she felt very dizzy and sick and she could not get up. The woman next to her held her hand. "My child, you have fever?"

Achola did not protest – she just leaned on the woman while the clergyman waded through numerous other announcements. When Achola gained her strength, people had started leaving the churchyard. The woman was still holding her hand. She decided quickly what to tell her. "Thank you mother, I felt suddenly sick, I think, I have malaria coming. I feel all right now, I will go home right away and swallow some quinine."

The woman looked at her – she had stopped sweating and she looked better.

"Go in peace, my child," the woman told her. Achola moved quietly from the church and walked straight home. She was surprised she reached the house safely, because she could not remember having crossed any road. Yet she must have followed the same dangerous road full of recklessly driven cars. She entered the house and ransacked the whole place – after about half an hour a heap of Owila's photographs lay piled high on a metal tray. Finally she brought the life-size one that stood near her bed and threw it on the heap without looking at it. The picture landed on the heap with the top facing upwards and the frame and glass intact.

Achola madly searched for a box of matches. She found it. She went to the store and brought out a tin of paraffin. She struggled to open the tin but it would not open. She put a cloth over it – still it would not open. Anger mounted in her; she threw the tin aside. She struck the match, it made a funny sound – the whole box was dripping wet and would not light. She had carelessly left it near the sink when she went to church and it had soaked up water. Achola stood with a wet matchbox in her hands staring at the heap of photographs before her. Then as if she had remembered something, she threw the matchbox away and grabbed the huge picture as if it were alive. She rubbed it violently on her chest, on her breasts, longing for the glass to break and pierce her heart: that was where Rapudo belonged. She was exhausted but she seemed possessed. She flopped on a chair, still clutching the photograph.

The afternoon was cool. People were walking towards the town. Sunday was a favourite day for sight-seeing and window-shopping in Kisumu. Young people from Nyalenda Village were laughing and talking at the top of their voices. They were coming towards her. She took a small path to avoid them. Some of them might be her students. Perhaps they would not recognise her. She had changed into a dirty old dress, she wore old slippers and she had covered her head and part of her face with a black scarf like a Nubian girl.

People were drinking and singing in the village. She mingled with the crowd that was walking towards the bar. She passed the first row of houses and the second. Where exactly was the house? Could she ask? No, she moved to the third row and turned into Odiaga Lane. That must be it, or at least it looked like it. A red tin-roofed house with a white door. She gathered all her courage and knocked at the door. Presently the door opened and an elderly lady in a white gown stood before her.

"Come in, my child," the woman's voice was very soft. Achola lowered the cloth so that the woman could not see her face and followed her into the inner room which was spacious and lighter than the outer one. The lady sat on an easy chair. She took a small stool beside her and offered it to the visitor. Achola sat on it, her face was still covered and tears ran along her cheeks. The old lady moved closer to her and removed the cloth from her face. The beauty and the tenderness of Achola's youth startled her. She had not had such a young customer for a very long time. She held Achola's face in her hands and searched her eyes pitifully.

"My child, what brings you to me at such a tender age?" Her voice was soft, almost a whisper. Achola opened her mouth to speak but her sobbing got louder till she could not listen.

"All right, weep as long as you like – when you finish, tell me your mission."

After a long time of weeping, Achola faced the old woman. "Now speak," the old woman looked away from her.

"I have lost the man I have loved all my life. I know I cannot live without him."

"Do you want to die then?"

"No, mother. I must not die because Rapudo, needs me. I want him to marry me. I want to live with him and look after him."

"But you have just told me that you have lost him. How can you marry him?"

"Mother," Achola burst out into tears again, "that is why I have come to you. Is there nothing you can do?" Silence. Achola's eyes searched the older woman's face. "How have you suddenly known that you have lost this man if you have loved him all your life?"

"I went to …" Achola stammered, now afraid to tell the old lady the truth.

"Carry on," the old lady encouraged her.

"In the church this morning, the clergyman announced that he is to marry another woman - in three weeks' time. Oh Mother, I nearly collapsed in the church. I wanted to stop him signing the register because Rapudo is mine, but by the time I had gained strength, he had signed it. We quarrelled one night four months ago, and a week later, he was transferred to Bondo Division. Though I have prayed daily he has never written to me, but I kept on hoping. Then today I got the shock."

"So you are a Christian?"

"Yes," Achola looked at her suspiciously.

"Will your parents be happy to know that you are here?"

"That I do not know – but I want you to help me, mother – that is why I am here. Please do not send me away."

"No, my child, I shall not send you away. I also work through God. I am His prophetess. He has given me power to see things that will happen and I am given the power to avert danger if I am warned in time. But many Christians do not believe in me. Yet they see my works daily."

"Mother," Achola looked at the prophetess eagerly, "do you think you can avert the wedding? Say you can do something to turn Rapudo's mind from this girl."

"But you have hardly given me enough time, my child. The wedding is already announced publicly. It will need drastic measures and quick action. But I want to be sure if you can keep a promise and if you can do exactly what I tell you."

"I will do everything you tell me, mother – anything that will make me marry Rapudo, not physically perhaps but if I can marry him in my heart that I may have something to live for."

"All right I am willing to help you. Now tell me frankly why you quarrelled – that will help me in my work."

"Mother, it was not a big thing," Achola said tearfully.

"However small, I must know."

"Well," Achola cleared her throat. "He wanted us to know each other before our marriage. But I would not, Mother. I wanted to honour my mother." Achola hid her face from the old lady. Perhaps she had said too much. For a while the prophetess stroked Achola's neck. Then she lifted her eyes and spoke to her. "Listen, my child, there is nothing to be sorry about. You are a noble woman. Unlike other educated women you have not taken to the white man's way. The God of our ancestors will reward you."

She brought out an old Bible from under the chair and placed it on her lap.

"Now put both hands over this," she told Achola.

Achola obeyed.

"Close your eyes."

Achola, obeyed.

"Say the words after me."

"I promise that I will strictly act on your word and that what we have discussed will remain a secret between the two of us. Amen."

Achola repeated the words after her. When she opened her eyes, the old lady smiled at her.

"Go in peace now. Come and see me after 19 days. When you come you will stay with me for two days. Tell no one where you are going. Should the headmaster press you, tell him that you are going to see your ailing mother. And remember keep your mouth shut and be back here on the 19th day."

As Achola left the prophetess' house she lowered the black cloth over her face so that nobody would recognise her. She hurried back to the school. The afternoon was far spent. She bathed and changed her clothes and, although she was not hungry, she forced down some food. A strange kind of peace flowed into her heart, a peace that she had not known for many weeks. Although the prophetess had not given her any sign of what she would do, somehow she trusted her. That night Achola slept soundly without weeping for Rapudo.

The school opened on Monday.

The last term was the busiest, with the countrywide examinations approaching. Achola threw herself wholeheartedly into work. The other members of staff had been told that Owila was to marry not Achola his longstanding girlfriend whom the whole school knew, but a girl from Yimbo Location. Knowing how much Achola loved Owila, none of them had the courage to ask her if she had heard the news. The weeks slipped by and Achola stayed out of church on Sundays. She pinned a calendar on top of her bed and each night before she went to sleep she put a cross over the figures to mark the end of a day.

The town was full of rumours about the coming wedding.

"What a beautiful girl for a man to leave," people said. Owila refused to discuss why he was jilting the girl like that to marry some girl from the bush whom he had only known for three months.

John and Jenny were upset to hear the news, but Owila refused to discuss why he was jilting the girl he had loved for so many years. Achola blocked her ears to rumours and avoided places where people could ask her awkward questions.

Then the 19th day of the month came. It was a Friday. After the morning lessons, Achola told the headmaster that she would be away for the weekend. Her mother was unwell and she would return on Monday by the early bus which passed near Pap Ndege School at 6.00 am. The headmaster gave her leave without further inquiries. In a way he was relieved to see Achola go out of town over the weekend. The staff had all been invited to the wedding and although they had blamed Owila for having dropped Achola most of them had accepted the invitation. To have Achola around at such a time would only be embarrassing.

By mid-afternoon Achola stood trembling at the prophetess' door. A black cloth covered her face. She did not mind what means the prophetess was going to use to avert the wedding, so long as Rapudo was safe to marry her one day. She had no particular thoughts about the other girl. She did not know her, she did not care for her and if she had allowed Rapudo to go to bed with her, then she was not worth ten cents or a wedding in the church.

The door opened unexpectedly and she went in. "I am glad you have kept your word," the prophetess told her.

"I always keep promises," Achola answered shyly.

The prophetess took Achola into a small bedroom which she told her would be hers while she stayed with her.

Have a little rest now. In the evening, I will talk to you."

At 8.00 pm. when supper had been served, the prophetess called Achola into her room to speak to her.

"Listen, my child. I want you to make a small present for Owila. I will tell you later how to get it to him. This is what I want you to sew for him."

She pulled out two white pillow cases which were richly embroidered on one side only.

"You are educated, I know you can sew. I want you to finish the work completely by tomorrow night before supper. On Sunday you and I will go on a long journey for a few days and when we come back from the journey, things will be different. Is that acceptable?"

"Yes, Mother, I can do anything for him. I can start tonight."

"No, tonight you must sleep."

Achola was puzzled at the prophetess' arrangements. A numb feeling in her heart mocked her, seeming to tell her that the wedding would not be called off, but somehow the prophetess' face reassured her. She slept badly. Her nagging fears, coupled with the unusual surroundings made the night drag.

So Achola settled down and started sewing the following morning. She worked solidly without interruption except for a few minutes at lunch time. By supper two pillow cases were beautifully embroidered. Achola was exhausted and her fingers were numb from continuous sewing. Her neck was stiff, and a pain on her back bothered her.

The older woman said, "Now have a bath and sleep. We are starting early in the morning."

Achola was so exhausted that when she slept she did not even turn over. She woke up with a start when the prophetess tiptoed into her room.

"It is all right, I did not want to wake you early but you must move fast. First have a good bath then have your food – it is ready. When you finish, tell me."

Achola moved swiftly but quietly. She was now excited, but not the kind of excitement she had had before. Her mother came to her mind, and she lowered her eyes sadly. She knew her mother would not approve of her seeking the prophetess' advice. Yet she had gone too far now. She would go through with it and explain to her later. She was sitting at the edge of her bed when the prophetess called her. Achola followed her into her own bedroom. The door was shut. The prophetess turned and faced Achola.

"Promise once more you will do everything I tell you before we go on the journey."

"Mother, she burst into tears. I thought by now you would trust me."

"No room for tears, my child," the prophetess told her sternly. "Our journey will be very tedious. I must be sure." There was no trace of kindness on her face now, only hard business.

"I am sorry, Mother. I will obey."

The prophetess then flung the door open and stood aside looking at her. Achola's heart stopped completely. If it was beating, she did not hear it. Little drops of perspiration formed over her nose and her forehead.

"Come," the prophetess beckoned her, but her feet were numb and heavy. She just stared with her mouth open.

"Can I still trust you?" The prophetess asked her now with a smile.

"Yes … Mother." The words simply dropped out of her mouth.

"Then come; there is little time."

Achola dragged her weary legs into the room. The two bridesmaids stood aside fully dressed. A long bridal gown was spread over the prophetess' bed and its whiteness made Achola blink several times. The prophetess dressed Achola quickly while she stood like a statue. Her mind was completely blank. If she tried to think she would weep. The dress fitted her perfectly as if it was measured on her. Then the prophetess took the white veil and put it over her as all brides did. The part of the veil covering the front head had two layers. Then she slipped the bridal shoes onto Achola's feet.

"Now listen, my child. The wedding is at 10.00 am. The car will get you to the church five minutes before the time. Nashon will go with you. Do not hesitate to enter. When you hear the sound of the organ walk gracefully towards the aisle. The groom will be waiting for you."

"But, Mother, whom am I marrying?" Achola panicked. If the prophetess cheated her and fooled her to marry another man, she would break her Bible oath and die.

"You are marrying Owila." The prophetess gripped her hands – because they were trembling.

"I am marrying Owila," Achola said breathlessly. "But how, Mother – what of the other bride?"

"I have planned everything perfectly. Kadimo is very far, my messenger told me that the bride was leaving her mother's house at 5.00 pm so as to be here by 9.00 am, but they will not make it. It rained heavily on that side and the roads are very sticky. I can see them now, they are having a bad time on the road. By the time she arrives the ceremony will be almost through.'

Achola's hands had not stopped trembling – she had tried to imagine the whole plan – but fear stopped her.

"But Rapudo will recognise me mother, and then … and then …"

"Just trust in me. Owila will not recognise you till after the ceremony, then even if he does not want to marry you physically, you will be married to him in your heart.

You will be bound to him. Now forget about the other girl and only think about yourself. My heart will go with you."

The two black cars stood waiting adorned with flowers. People standing by assumed that this was just another bride going to meet her man. They had seen so many bridal cars and there was nothing unusual about it.

Achola was helped into the first car by the man called Nashon. The little bridesmaids sat with her, one on each side – each holding a little white bouquet. The prophetess stood at the door with her hands clasped over her chest. Achola caught a glimpse of her through her double veil and her heart felt at peace. Then the cars moved away.

St. Peter's Church was packed with friends and relatives of the bride and groom. Two candles were burning brightly at the altar. Reverend Omach and Father Hussen stood wearing their white and black robes. The groom with his best man stood in front with white flowers in their button holes. The congregation sat quietly listening to the soft organ music. Owila was a little nervous – he had had a hectic week with numerous arrangements to make. The District Commissioner had given him 10 days off as part of his holidays. He would make use of those 10 days to know his wife better, because quite frankly, things had happened so hurriedly that he had not had a chance to know her well.

The few people who were still talking outside the church rushed in to find their places and the whispers filled the church. "The bride has arrived."

As the bride stepped into the entrance of the church the organ boomed out, 'Here comes the bride', and the people got up to honour the bride and her maids. Achola walked gracefully towards the aisle. Owila had turned round and now found her. The sight of him nearly made Achola topple over; she had not seen him for four months. Her heart ached so much that she felt something wet running about her cheeks.

"No, Owila could never belong to that other woman. He is mine." Owila had met her, they were standing side by side now. Then they walked up the aisle following Reverend Omach who led them. Achola felt Owila's shoulders rubbing against hers as they knelt together on the cushions before Father Hussen. Old memories filled her heart strengthening her to go through with it.

The hymn ended and Father Hussen's voice filled the church and the solemn swearing of, 'Will thou have this woman to be thy wedded wife' started.

Achola listened to the words attentively, but her heart was drumming away in her ears at the thought that soon Father Hussen would call upon her to repeat those very words and Owila might recognise her voice. She gripped hard on the rail to stop her hands from trembling. She heard Owila's voice saying, "I will," and then Father Hussen, faced her. "You, Felomena Wariwa, wilt thou have this man to be thy wedded husband?" Achola swallowed and then said faintly, "I will."

A cold breeze swept through the church. The congregation was attentive. Some of the couples who had been married for many years listened to these strange words from the priest with renewed passion. Jenny Hannington pressed John's hand and whispered, "I can't wait to see this woman's face, I am dying to set my eyes on her. I suppose she is very beautiful to have swept Owila off his feet just like that."

"Well, people around Kisumu know very little about her. I bet they are all dying to see her."

"They say she is just from the bush, no roads, no shops, and yet, John, she is so beautifully dressed and carries herself like a queen."

"I don't care, Jenny, I think the other woman whom Owila jilted is a star." John strained his eyes at the crowd not really expecting to see Achola there, just restless. Then he whispered to Jenny, "She can't be here, she must be so broken-hearted."

Owila hesitated as he pronounced the words, "Till death do us part." He had always felt that a Christian marriage was committing a man too far, but he suppressed the thought. So many other men had gone through the ordeal. Maybe a new generation will revise the prayer-book and leave these words 'till death' out. He let go of the bride's hand, and on the direction of Father Hussen, Achola took Owila's right hand in her right hand and repeated the same words after Father Hussen.

"I, Felomena Wariwa, take thee, Absalom Owila, to be my wedded husband."

Achola's faint voice trembled away as she struggled to say the words after Father Hussen. Owila just managed to hear the words, but that satisfied him. He as a man had found those words heavy and strenuous to say – he could not blame his bride for being afraid. Then the ring was placed on the book of God for the blessing. Father Hussen took the ring and gave it to Owila and asked him to place it on the fourth finger of the bride's left hand. Owila held the ring tenderly and followed the words:

"With this ring I thee wed, with my body, I thee worship and with my worldly goods I thee endow. In the name of the Father and of the Son and of the Holy Ghost. Amen!'

Owila felt hot under the arms and could feel the perspiration pouring down on his side. Was he afraid? No, he was just excited. To get married and to wade through all these ominous words was not easy. A devilish mask of Achola, the girl whom he once loved so much flashed through his mind – appeared without a warning, and the perspiration under his arm increased, but he shook her out of his mind. He was a married man now and when in the arms of his bride, he would forget Achola completely. Yes, it was just a matter of time. Then Father Hussen pronounced:

"These whom God has joined together let no man put asunder." And Father Hussen eyed the congregation critically and told them, "For as much as Absalom and Felomena have consented together in holy wedlock and have witnessed the same before God and this company, and thereto have pledged their troth either to the other, and have declared the same by giving and receiving of a ring and by joining of hands, I pronounce that they be Man and Wife together, in the name of the Father and of the Son and of the Holy Ghost. Amen."

But Father Hussen's last words were drowned by a murmuring that broke out from the congregation. Father Hussen adjusted his glasses to focus and his eyes rested on the Reverend Omach's open mouth. A bride and twelve bridesmaids were walking along the path towards the aisle. Yes, they were halfway along the aisle. The congregation was now out of control and all talking loudly.

A woman's voice called, "Can't someone do something?"

Another voice shouted, "There must be a mistake."

The growing confusion brought the bridal procession to a halt. Father Hussen stood at the altar shouting at the top of his voice, "Order, Order! My children, Order!"

The congregation responded to his trembling voice and there was silence in the church. Father Hussen then walked towards the bridal party. He stood before the bride and asked her aloud, "My daughter, you must be in the wrong place. We are in the middle of another wedding. And whom are you marrying, my daughter?"

"Absalom Owila."

The shrill emotional bridal voice echoed through the church, and the people who sat in the front pew heard the words quite distinctly. For a minute or so there was dead silence. Then an insistent murmuring broke out again in the congregation. Father Hussen walked back to the altar where Owila was still kneeling besides his bride. He removed the double veil from the bride's face and Owila came face to face with the girl who had just been proclaimed his wife. Owila disentangled his arm from the woman kneeling besides him. Either he was dreaming or he had gone off his head. Achola's tearful eyes were fixed on him.

"But Father, Father …" Owila staggered to his feet.

"She is not my bride. She is …" And Owila turned round to face the congregation and there before him stood Felomena – the girl he was supposed to marry, with her bridesmaids. He staggered down to her, but Father Hussen barred his way.

"My son, you cannot go to her and leave your wife here. You are married to this woman now!"

"No, no, no," Owila shouted. "Do something, Father, please."

"Not now, my son, the solemn promise you had both said to one another is binding."

The congregation was out of control again. Some were shouting, others were weeping around the woman who had fainted before them. Owila turned round to look at Achola but the woman in the white bridal gown was nowhere to be seen. He broke loose and hurried towards the crowd but they barred his way and he could not see Felomena or her bridesmaids. He shouted to them to give him way. But his voice was drowned by the crowd, like a man cut off from help in a nightmare.

At the altar Achola was sobbing before Father Hussen. "He is mine. I have loved him all my life – I will serve him all my life. He is mine." And Father Hussen went down and tapped on Owila's shoulder.

"My son, your wife is waiting for you."

Study Questions

1. In note form, describe the main episodes that make up the plot of the story.
2. What point of view is used in this story? Explain its effectiveness.
3. Comment on the writer's use of any three literary devices in the story.
4. Describe the characters of Achola, Owila, John and Miss Hannington comparatively.

Something Old, Something New

Leila Aboulela

Her country disturbed him. It reminded him of the first time he had held a human bone; the touching simplicity of it, the strength. Such was the landscape of Khartoum: bone-coloured sky, a purity in the desert air, bareness. A bit austere and therefore static. But he was driven by feelings, that was why he was here, that was why he had crossed boundaries and seas, and now walked through a blaze of hot air from the aeroplane steps to the terminal.

She was waiting for him outside the airport, wearing the national dress; a pale orange robe that made her look even more slender than she was.

"I mustn't kiss you."

"No," she laughed, "you mustn't."

He had forgotten how vibrant she was, how happy she made him feel. She talked, asked him questions. Did you have a good trip? Are you hungry? Did all your luggage arrive? Were they nice to you in the customs? I missed you too. There was a catch in her voice when she said that; in spite of her confidence, she was shy.

"Come, come and meet my brother." They began to walk across a car park that was disorganised and dusty, the sun gleaming on the cars.

Her brother was leaning against a dilapidated Toyota. He was lanky with a hard-done-by expression. He looked irritated. Perhaps by the conflicting desire to get his sister off his hands and his misgivings about her marrying a foreigner. How did he see him now, through those narrow eyes, how did he judge him?

A European coming to shake his hand, murmuring *salamu alleikum*, predictably wearing jeans, a white shirt, but somewhat subdued for a foreigner

She sat in the front next to her brother. He sat in the back with the rucksack that wouldn't fit in the boot. The car seats were shabby, a thin film of dust covered everything. I will get used to the dust, he told himself, but not the heat. He could do with a breath of fresh air, that tang of rain he was accustomed to. He wanted her to be next to him. And it suddenly seemed to him, in a peevish sort of way, unfair that they should be separated like that. She turned her head back and looked at him, smiled as if she knew. He wanted to say, "You have no idea how much I ache for you, you have no idea." But he could not say that, not least because the brother understood English. It was like a ride in a fun-fair. The windows wide open; voices, noises, car-horns, people crossing the road at random, pausing in the middle, touching the cars with their fingers as if the cars were benign cattle. Anyone of these passers-by could easily punch him through the window, yank off his watch, his sun-glasses, snatch his wallet from the pocket of his shirt. He tried to roll up the window but couldn't. She turned and said, "It's broken, I'm sorry." Her calmness made him feel that he needn't be so nervous. A group of school-boys walked on the pavement, one of them stared at him, grinned and waved. He became aware that everyone looked like her, shared her colour, the women were dressed like her and they walked with the same slowness which had seemed to him exotic when he had seen her walking in Edinburgh. "Everything is new for you," she turned and looked at him gently. The brother said something in Arabic.

The car moved away from the crowded market to a wide shady road.

"Look!" she said, "take off your sun-glasses and look. There's the Nile." And there was the Nile, a blue he had never seen before, a child's blue, a dream's blue.

"Do you like it?" she asked. She was proud of her Nile.

"Yes, it's beautiful," he replied. But as he spoke he noticed that the river's flow was forceful, not innocent, not playful. Crocodiles no doubt lurked beneath the surface, hungry and ruthless. He could picture an accident; blood, death, bones.

"And here is your hotel," she said. "I booked you in the Hilton." She was proud that her country had a Hilton.

The car swept up the drive. A porter in a gaudy green uniform and stiff turban opened the door for him before he could do it himself. The porter took his rucksack. There was a small fuss involving her brother in order to open the boot and get the suitcase. His luggage was mostly presents for her family. She had told him on the phone what to get and how much to get. They would be offended, she had explained, if you come empty handed, they would think you don't care for me enough.

The hotel lobby was impressive, the cool tingling blast of the air-conditioner, music playing, an expanse of marble. He felt soothed somehow, more in control, after the bumpy ride. With her brother away parking the car and a queue at the reception desk, they suddenly had time to talk.

"I need an exit visa," she explained, "to be able to leave and go back with you. To get the exit visa, I have to give a reason for leaving the country."

"Because you're my wife," he said and they smiled at the word. "Will be my wife. Will be *Insha' Allah.*"

"*Insha'Allah.*"

"That's it,' she said, 'we won't be able to get married and just leave. We'll have to stay a few days till the papers get sorted out. And the British Embassy … that's another story."

"I don't understand what the problem is," he said.

"Oh," she sighed, "people have a wedding and they go off on their honeymoon. But we won't be able to do that, we will have to hang around and run from the Ministry of Interior to the Passport Office to the British Embassy."

102

"I see," he said. "I see. Do I need an exit visa?"

"No, you're a visitor. You can leave whenever you like. But I need a visa. I need a reason to leave."

"Right."

They looked at each other and then he said, 'I don't think your brother likes me."

"No, no he doesn't mean to be unfriendly ... you'll see." The first time he saw her was at the Sudanese restaurant near the new mosque in Edinburgh. His old Chemistry teacher had taken him there after Friday prayers. When she brought the menu, she told them that the peanut soup was good – a specialty - but his teacher wanted the humus salad and he ordered the lentil soup instead because it was familiar. He was cautious by nature, wanting new things but held back by a vague mistrust. It was enough for the time being that he had stepped into the Nile Cafe, he had no intention of experimenting with weird tastes.

He was conscious of her footsteps as she came from the kitchen, up the stairs. She was wearing trousers and a brown headscarf that was tied at the back of her neck. She had very black eyes that slanted. After that day he went to the Nile Cafe alone and often. It was convenient, close to the Department of Zoology where he worked as a lab technician. He wondered if, as she leaned to put the dish of couscous in front of him, she could smell the chemicals on him.

They got talking because there weren't many customers in the restaurant and she had time on her hands. The restaurant was new and word had not yet got round that it was good.

"We've started to get a few people coming in from the mosque," she told him, "Friday especially is a good day." "Yes, it was a Friday when I first came here and met you." She smiled in a friendly way. He told her that at one time he had not known that the big building next to the restaurant was a mosque. There was no sign that said so.

"I thought it was a church," he said and she laughed and laughed. He left her an extra tip that day; it was not often that people laughed at his jokes.

Had it not been for his old Chemistry teacher he would never have gone to the mosque. At a bus stop, he had recognised a face he had not seen for a number of years; a face associated with a positive feeling, a time of encouragement – secondary school, the ease with which he had written lab reports. They recognised each other straight away. "How are you? What are you doing now? You were my best student."

In primary and secondary school, he had been the brightest in his class, the most able. He sat for the three sciences in his Standard Grades and got three As. It was the same when he did his Highers. There was no reason at all, his teachers said, why he should not sail through medical school. But he got to his third year in Medicine and failed, failed again and dropped out. He had counselling and his parents were supportive, but no one ever really understood what had gone wrong. He was as bewildered by his failure as everyone else was. His get-up-and-go had suddenly disappeared, as if amputated. "What's it all for, what's the point?" he asked himself. He asked himself the taboo questions. And really, that was the worst of it; these were the questions that brought all the walls down.

Snap out of it, he was told, and snap out of it he eventually did. A girlfriend helped but then she found a job in London and drifted away. He was simply not up to medical school. It's a shame, everyone agreed. They were sympathetic but at the same time they labelled him now, they put him in a box, a student who had 'dropped-out', a 'giver-upper'.

One day when she brought him his plate of aubergine and mince meat he asked her, "Would you like to go up to Arthur's Seat?" She had never been there before. It was windy, a summer wind that carried away the hats of tourists and messed up people's hair. Because her hair was covered, she looked neat, slightly apart from everyone else. It made the outing not as carefree as he imagined it would be. She told him she had recently got divorced after six months of marriage. She laughed when she said six months not six years, but he could tell she was sore – it was in her eyes.

"You have beautiful eyes," he said.

"Everyone tells me that," she replied. He flushed and looked away at the green and grey houses that made up Edinburgh. She had wanted to talk about her divorce; she had not wanted to hear compliments.

They talked a little about the castle. He told her about his girlfriend, not the nice one who had gone down south, but the previous one who had dumped him. He was able to laugh about it now. She said her husband had married her against his will. Not against her will, she stressed, but his will.

"He was in love with an English girl but his family disapproved and stopped sending the money he needed to continue his studies in Edinburgh. They thought a Sudanese girl like me would make him forget the girlfriend he had been living with. They were wrong. Everything went wrong from day one. It's a stupid story," she said her hands in her pockets. "Did you love him?" he asked her. Yes, she had loved him, wanted to love him. She had not known about his English girlfriend. After the honeymoon, when he brought her to Edinburgh and started acting strange, she asked him and he told her everything.

"Would you believe it," she said, "his family now blames me for the divorce! They say I wasn't clever enough, I didn't try hard enough. They're going around Khartoum saying all these things about me. That's why I don't want to go back. But I'll have to eventually when my visa runs out."

"I'm glad I'm not pregnant," she went on. "I thank Allah every day that I didn't become pregnant."

After that they spoke about faith. He told her how he had become a Muslim. He spoke about his former Chemistry teacher – how, after meeting again, they had fallen back into the swing of their old teacher-student relationship. She listened, fascinated. She asked him questions.

"What was your religion before?"

"I was a Catholic."

"Have you always believed in God?"

"Yes."

"Why on earth did you convert?"

She seemed almost surprised by his answers. She associated Islam with her dark skin, her African blood, her own weakness. She couldn't really understand why anyone like him would want to join the wretched of the world. But he spoke with warmth. It made her look at him properly, as if for the first time.

"Your parents probably don't like it," she said, "or your friends? They won't like you changing." She was candid in that way. And she was right. He had lost one friend after a bitter, unnecessary argument; another withdrew. His parents struggled to hide their dismay. Ever since he had dropped out of medical school, they had feared for his well-being, fretted that he would get sucked up into unemployment, drugs, depression; the underworld that throbbed and dragged itself parallel to their active middle-class life. Only last week, their neighbour's son had hanged himself (drugs of course and days without showering). There was a secret plague that targeted young men.

Despite their misgivings about his conversion to Islam, his parents eventually had to admit that he looked well; he put on a bit of weight, got a raise at work. If only he would not talk about religion. They did not understand that side of him that was theoretical, intangible, belonging to the spiritual world. If only he would not mention religion then it would be easier to pretend that nothing had changed. He was confident enough to humour them. Elated that the questions he had once asked – what's it all for, what does it all mean, what's the point of going on – the questions that had tilted the walls around him and nearly smothered him, were now valid. They were questions that had answers, answers that provoked other questions, that opened new doors, that urged him to look at things in another way like holding a cube in his hand, turning it round and round, or like moving around a tall column and looking at it from the other side, how different it was and how the same.

When he took her to meet his parents, the afternoon was a huge success. We're going to get married he said, and there a kind of relief in his mother's eyes. It was easier for his parents to accept that he was in love with a Muslim girl than it was to accept that he was in love with Islam.

From the balcony of his hotel room, he looked out at the Blue Nile. Sunshine so bright that he saw strands of shimmering light. Palm trees, boats, the river was so blue. Would the water be cool, he wondered, or tepid? He felt sleepy. The telephone rang and he went indoors again, sliding the tinted glass door behind him.

Her happy voice again. "What were you doing, why aren't you asleep? Everyone sleeps this time in the afternoon, it's siesta time, you must be exhausted. Did you remember to bring dollar bills – not sterling, not traveller cheques? You mustn't eat at the hotel, it will he terribly expensive, you must eat only with us here at home. Yes, we'll pick you up later. You'll come for dinner, you'll meet my parents. Don't forget the gifts. Are you going to dream of me?"

He dreamt that he was still on the aeroplane. He woke up an hour later, thirsty, looked up and saw a small arrow painted on the ceiling of the room. What was the arrow for? Out on the balcony, the contrast startled him. Sunset had softened the sky, rimmed the West with pinks and soft orange. The Nile was benign, the sky already revealing a few stars, the air fresher. Birds swooped and zigzagged.

He heard the *azan*; the first time in his life to hear it outdoors. It was not as spectacular as he had thought it would be, not as sudden. It seemed to blend with the sound of the birds and the changing sky. He started to figure out the direction of Makkah using the setting sun as his guide. Straight East or even a little to the North-East it would be now, not south-east as it was from Scotland. He located the East and when he went back into the room, understood the purpose of the arrow that was painted on the ceiling. The arrow was to show the hotel guests which way to face Makkah. After he had prayed, he went downstairs and looked for the swimming pool. He swam in water that was warm and pungent with chlorine. Twilight was swift. In no time the sky turned a dark purple with sharp little stars. It was the first time he had swum under a night sky.

Her house was larger than he had imagined, shabbier. It was full of people – she had five brothers and sisters, several nephews and nieces, an uncle who looked like an older, smaller version of Bill Cosby and an aunt who was asleep on a string bed in the corner of the room. The television blared. Her mother smiled at him and offered him sweets. Her father talked to him in careful, broken English. Everyone stared at him, curious, pleased. Only the brother looking bored, stretched out on another string bed staring at the ceiling.

"So now you've seen my family," she said, naming her sisters, her nieces and nephews. The names swam in his head. He smiled and smiled until he strained the muscles of his face. "Now you've seen where I grew up," she said, as if they had got over a hurdle. He realised, for the first time, the things she'd never had: a desk of her own, a room of her own, her own cupboard, her own dressing table, her own mug, her own packet of biscuits. She had always lived as part of a group, part of her family. What that was like, he didn't know. He did not know her well enough. He had yet to see her hair, he had yet to know what she looked like when she cried and what she looked like when she woke up in the morning.

"After we have had dinner," she said, "my uncle knows an English song," she was laughing again, sitting on the arm of the sofa. "He wants to sing it for you."

Bill Cosby's look-a-like sat up straight in his armchair and sang, *"Cricket, lovely cricket at Lords where I saw it. Cricket, lovely cricket at Lords where I saw it."*

Everyone laughed. After singing, the uncle was out of breath.

They went on outings which she organised. They went on a boat trip, a picnic in the forest, they visited the camel market. On each of these outings, they were accompanied by her brother, her sisters, her nephews and nieces, her girlfriends.

They were never alone. He remembered Michael in *The Godfather,* climbing the hills of Italy with his fiancé, surrounded by armed guards and her numerous relatives, backed by an unforgettable soundtrack. It was like that but without the guns. And instead of rolling hills, there was flat scrubland, the edges of a desert. He watched her, how she carried a nephew, how she smiled, how she peeled a grapefruit and gave him a piece to eat, how she giggled with her girlfriends. He took lots of photographs. She gave him strange fruits to eat. One was called *doum* and it was brown, large as an orange, almost hard as rock, with a woody taste and a straw-like texture. Only the thin outer layer was to be gnawed at and chewed, most of it was the stone. Another fruit was called *gongoleez*, sour, tangy, white chunks, chalky in texture to suck on and throw the black stones away. Tamarind to drink, *kerkadah* to drink, *turmus, kebkebeh, nabaq.* Peanut salad, stuffed aubergines, *moulah, kisra, waikah, moiiloukhia.* Dishes he had eaten before in the Nile Cafe, dishes that were new. She never tired of saying to him, "Here, taste this, it's nice, try this!"

"Can't we be alone, just for a bit?" he appealed.

"My family is very strict, especially because I'm divorced; they're very strict," she said but her eyes were smiling.

"Try and sort something out."

"Next week after the wedding, you'll see me every day and get tired of me."

"You know I can't ever get tired of you!" he exclaimed.

"How can I know that?" She smiled.

She could flirt for hours given the chance. Now there was no chance because it was not clear whether her uncle, Bill Cosby, eyes closed and head nodding forward, was dozing in his armchair or eavesdropping.

Mid-morning in Ghamhouriah Street, after they had bought ebony to take back to his parents, he felt a tug on his shoulder, turned and found his rucksack slashed open, his passport missing; his camera too. He started to shout.

"Calm down," she said, but he could not calm down. It was not only anger – there was plenty of that – but the eruption of latent fears, the slap of a nightmare. Her brother had parked the car in a bit of shade in a side street. They reached it, her brother tenser than ever, she downcast and he clutching his ravaged rucksack. He kicked the tyre of the car, f-this and f-that. Furious he was, and out to abuse the place, the time, the crime. The whole street stood still and watched a foreigner go berserk, as if they were watching a scene in an American movie. A car drove past and the driver craned his neck to get a better look, laughed.

"Please," she said, "stop it, you're embarrassing me." He did not hear her. Her voice could not compete with the roar of anger in his ears.

"We'll have to go to the British Embassy and get him a new passport," she said to her brother.

"No, we'll have to go to the police station and report this first," he replied, getting into the car, wiping the sweat on his forehead with his sleeves.

"Get in the car," she said to him. "We'll have to go to the police station and report your stolen passport."

He got into the car, fuming.

The police station was surprisingly pleasant: a bungalow and several outbuildings. It was shady, cool. They were treated well, given cold water, tea. He refused to drink the tea, sat in a sulk.

"Do you know how much that camera cost?" he hissed. "And it's not insured."

She shrugged, less shocked by what had happened than he was. Soothed by the drink, she started to tease him.

"They'll chop off the hand of the thief who stole your camera. Really they will." Her brother laughed with her.

"I really can't see what's so funny," he was still brooding.

"Can't you take a joke?" she said and there was an edge to her voice. Afterwards they drove in silence to the British Embassy. There, they endured a long queue. The Embassy staff hemed and hawed. They did not like to hear of passports getting stolen. And as one question led to the other, they were not overjoyed either to hear of people getting married in a few days' time. They interrogated her and her brother, broad, flat questions but still she felt sullied and small. Coming out of the embassy, she was anything but calm.

"What did they think? What were they trying to insinuate? That I stole your passport! As if I am desperate to go back there."

"What's that supposed to mean?" he asked.

"It's supposed to mean what it means! You think you're doing me a big favour by marrying me?"

"No, I don't think that, of course not … "

"They do! They do, the way they were talking. Sneering at me and you didn't even notice!"

"Okay, okay, calm down."

A small boy touched his arm, begging. Gnarled fist, black skin turned grey from malnutrition, one eye clogged with thick mucous.

He flinched at the unpleasant touch, felt guilty, fumbled in his pockets and started to take out a two-hundred dinar note.

"Are you out of your mind," she said, "giving him that amount? He'll get mugged for it." She opened her bag and gave the boy instead some coins and an orange.

As she got in the car, she told her brother about the beggar and they both laughed in a mocking way – laughing at him in Arabic, the height of rudeness.

"Perhaps you can contribute to the petrol then," the brother drawled, "given you have so much cash to spare. I've burnt a lot of gas chauffeuring you and your fiancé around, you know."

"Right, if this is what you want!" He yanked out the notes from his wallet and slammed them down near the handbrake.

"Thanks," her brother said, but when he picked the wad of cash, he looked at it like it was not much, like he had expected more. She sighed and looked out of the window. It was as if the theft had brought out all the badness in them. He thought of asking to be dropped at the hotel. He thought of giving up and leaving for Scotland the next day. That would punish her for laughing at him; that would hurt her. But he did not ask to be dropped off. He did not give up. True he had no passport and would not be able to travel, but something else made him stay.

They walked into disarray – her house, almost unrecognisable for the sheer number of people who were distraught, in shock. A woman was pushing the furniture to one side; another dropped a mattress on the floor; everywhere weeping, weeping and a few hoarse voices shouting orders. Her uncle, Bill Cosby's look-alike, had died, dozing in his armchair.

For a moment, the three of them stood in the middle of the room, frozen in disbelief. The brother started to ask questions in a loud voice.

"That's it," she hissed, "we'll never have our wedding now, not in the middle of this mourning, never, never!" And she burst into tears.

Before he could respond, her brother led him away, saying "The house will be for the women now, we have to go outside. Come on."

The garden was hell that time of day, sun scorching the grass, reflecting on the concrete slabs of the garage. How precious shade was in this part of the world, how quickly a quarrel could be pushed aside, how quickly the dead were taken to their graves. Where was he now, the uncle who sang, *'Cricket, lovely cricket!'* Somewhere indoors being washed with soap, perfumed and then wrapped in white, that was the end then, without preliminaries. He could faint standing in the sun like that, without a passport, without her, without the reassurance that their wedding would go ahead. It couldn't be true. But it was and minute after minute passed with him standing in the garden. Where was her brother now, who had previously watched his every move while she had circled him with attention, advice, plans? She was indoors sucked up in rituals of grief he knew nothing about. Well he could leave now, slip away unnoticed. He could walk to the main road and hail a taxi – something he had not done before because she and her brother had picked him up and dropped him back at the hotel every single day. Death, the destroyer of pleasures.

The body was being taken away. There it was shrouded in white and the shock of seeing that Bill Cosby face again, asleep, fast asleep. The folds of nostrils and lips, the pleasing contrast of white hair against dark skin. He found himself following her brother into the car, getting into what now had become his seat at the back, two men crammed in next to him, an elderly man sat in front. The short drive to the mosque, rows of men. He had prayed that special prayer for the dead once before in Edinburgh, for a still-born baby. It did not involve any kneeling, was brief, cool. Here it was also raw, the fans whirling down from the ceiling, the smell of sweat and haste.

They drove out of town to the cemetery. He no longer asked himself why he was accompanying them; it seemed the right thing to do. In the car, there was a new ease between them, a kind of bonding because they had prayed together. They began to talk of the funeral announcement that went out on the radio after the news, the obituaries that would be published in the newspaper the next day. He half-listened to the Arabic he could not understand, to the summary in English which one of them would suddenly give, remembering his presence.

Sandy wind blowing, a home that was flat ground, a home that had no walls, no doors. "My family's cemetery," her brother said suddenly addressing him. Once he married her and took her back with him to Edinburgh, would he be expected to bring her back here if she, God-forbid, died? Why think these miserable thoughts? A hole was eventually made in the ground; you would think they were enjoying the scooping out of dirt, so whole-heartedly were they digging. With the sleeve of his shirt, he wiped the sweat off his brow – he was beginning to act like them – since when did he wipe his face with his shirtsleeves in Edinburgh? He wanted a glass of cold water but they were lowering the uncle in the grave now. They put him in a niche, wedged him in so that when they filled the grave, the soil they poured in did not fall on him.

For the next three days, he sat in the tent that had been set up in the garden for the men. A kind of normality prevailed, people pouring in to pay their condolences, the women going indoors, the men to the tent. A flow of water glasses, coffee, tea, the buzz of flies. Rows of metal chairs became loose circles and knots, as old friends caught up with each other, a laugh here and there could be heard. "What's going to happen to your wedding now?" he was asked. He shrugged, he did not want to talk about it, was numbed by what had happened, dulled by the separation from her that the mourning customs seemed to impose. In the tent, the men agreed that the deceased had had a good death, no hospital, no pain, no intensive care and he was in his eighties, for God's sake, what more do you expect? A strange comfort in that tent. He fell into this new routine.

After breakfast in the hotel, he would walk along the Nile, and after passing the Presidential Palace, hail down a taxi, go to her house. He never met her and she never phoned him. After spending the day in the tent and having lunch with her brother and his friends, one of them would offer him a lift back to the Hilton.

Late in the evening or the early morning, he would go swimming. Every day he could hold his breath longer under water. When he went for a walk, he saw army trucks carrying young soldiers in green uniforms. The civil war in the South had gone on for years and wasn't drawing to an end – on the local television station there were patriotic songs, marches. He had thought, from the books he'd read and the particular British Islam he had been exposed to, that in a Muslim country he would find elegance and reason. Instead he found melancholy, a sensuous place, life stripped to the bare bones. On the third evening after the funeral, the tent was pulled down, the official mourning period was over.

"I want to talk to you," he said to her brother, "perhaps we could go for a walk?"

They walked in a street calmed by the impending sunset. Only a few cars passed. He said, "I can't stay here for long. I have to go back to my work in Scotland."

"I'm sorry," the brother said, "we could not have your wedding. But you understand."

"It's going to be difficult for me to come again. I think we should go ahead with our plans … "

"We can't celebrate at a time like this."

"It doesn't have to be a big celebration."

"You know, she had a big wedding party last time?"

"No, I didn't know. She didn't tell me."

"I blame myself," her brother suddenly blurted out, "that son of a dog and what he did to her! I knew, you see. I heard rumours that he was going with that girl but I didn't think much of it.

I thought it was just a fling he was having and he'd put his girlfriend away once he got married."

They walked in silence after that, the sound of their footsteps on crumbling asphalt. There was movement and voices in the houses around them, the rustle and barks of stray dogs. Finally her brother said, "I suppose we could have the marriage ceremony at my flat. But just the ceremony, no party … "

"No no, there's no need for a party … "

"I'll talk to my father and my mother, see if they approve the idea."

"Yes please, and after the ceremony … "

"After the ceremony you can take her back with you to your hotel … "

"Right."

"Her father has to agree first."

"Yes, of course." He walked lighter now, but there was still another hitch.

"You know," her brother said, "we lost a lot of money marrying her off to that son of a dog. A lot of money. And now again this time … even just for a simple ceremony at my place, I will have to buy drinks, sweets, pay for this and that."

On a street corner, money was exchanged between them. He handed her brother one fifty dollar bill after the other, not stopping until he sensed a saturation.

"Thanks, better not tell her about this, okay? My sister's always been sensitive and she doesn't realise how much things cost."

His hand trembled a little as he put his wallet away. He had previously paid a dowry (a modest one, the amount decided by her) and he had brought the gifts in good faith. Now he felt humiliated, as if he had been hoodwinked or as if he had been so insensitive as to underestimate his share in the costs. Or as if he had paid for her.

On the night before the wedding, he slept lightly, on and off, so the night seemed to him elongated, obtuse. At one time he dreamt of a vivid but unclear sadness and when he woke he wished that his parents were with him, wished that he was not alone, getting married all alone. Where were the stag night, the church wedding, invitation cards, a reception and speeches? His older brother had got married in church wearing the family kilt. It had been a sunny day and his mother had worn a blue hat. He remembered the unexpected sunshine, the photos. He had turned his back on these customs, returned them as if they were borrowed, not his. He had no regrets, but he had passed the stage of rejection now, burnt out the zeal of the new convert, was less proud, more ready to admit to himself what he missed. No, his parents could not have accompanied him. They were not hardy enough to cope with the heat, the mosquitoes, the maimed beggars in the street, all the harshness that even a good hotel could not shield. Leave them be, thank them now humbly in the dark for the generous cheque they had given him.

He dreamt he was being chased by the man who had ripped his rucksack, stolen his passport and camera. He woke up sweaty and thirsty. It was three in the morning, not yet dawn. He prayed, willing himself to concentrate, to focus on what he was saying, who he was saying it to. In this early hour of the morning, before the stir of dawn, all was still – even his mind which usually buzzed with activity, even his feelings which tumbled young. Just a precious stillness, patience, patience for the door to open, for the contact to be made, for the comforting closeness. He had heard a talk once at the mosque, that there are certain times of the day and the year when Allah answers prayers indiscriminately, fully, immediately – certain times – so who knows, you might one moment pray and be spot on, you might ask and straight away be given.

After dawn he slept and felt warm as if he had a fever. But he felt better when he woke late with the telephone ringing and her clear voice saying, "I'm so excited I'm going to be coming to the Hilton to stay with you. I've never stayed in a Hilton before, I can't wait." It was a matter of hours now.

Her brother's flat was in a newly built area, a little deserted, out of the way. One of her cousins had picked him up from the hotel and now they both shuffled up the stairs. The staircase was in sand, not yet laid out in tiles or concrete, there was a sharp smell of paint and bareness. The flat itself was neat and simple; a few potted plants, a large photograph of the *Ka'ba*. The men, her brother, father, various relations and neighbours whom he recognised from the days in the mourning tent, occupied the front room, the one near the door. The women were at the back of the flat. He couldn't see them, couldn't see her.

Shaking hands, the hum of a general conversation in another language. The Imam wore a white *jellabiya*, a brown cloak, a large turban. He led them for the *maghrib* prayer and after that the ceremony began. Only it was not much of a ceremony, but a signing of a contract between the groom and the bride's father. The Imam pushed away the dish of dates that was on the coffee table and started to fill out a form. The date in the Western calendar, the date in the Islamic calendar. The amount of dowry (the original figure she had named and not the additional dollars her brother had taken on the street corner). The name of the bride. The name of her father who was representing himself.

"But that is not a Muslim name." The Imam put the pen down, sat back in his chair.

"Show him your certificate from the mosque in Edinburgh," urged her brother, "the one you showed me when you first arrived."

"I can't," he said, "it was stolen or it fell out when the things in my bag were stolen."

"No matter," the brother sighed and turned to speak to the Imam. "He's a Muslim for sure. He prayed with us. Didn't you see him praying just now behind you?"

"Did they tell you I have eyes at the back of my head?" enquired the Iman.

Laughter … that didn't last long.

"Come on, sheikh," one of the guests said, "we're all gathered here for this marriage to take place *insha'Allah*. We've all seen this foreigner praying, not just now but also on the days of the funeral. Let's not start to make problems."

"Look, he will recite for you the *Fatiha*," the brother said, "won't you?" He put his hand on his shoulder as a way of encouragement.

"Come on, sheikh," another guest said, "these people aren't even celebrating or having a party. They're in difficult circumstances, don't make things more difficult. The bride's brother said he saw an official certificate; that should be enough."

"*Insha' Allah* there won't be any difficulties," someone ventured.

"Let him recite," the Imam said, looking away.

He was sweating now. No, not everyone's eyes were on him, some were looking away, hiding their amusement or feeling embarrassed on his behalf. He sat forward, his elbows on his knees.

"In the Name of Allah, the Compassionate, the Merciful," her brother whispered helpfully.

"In the Name of Allah, the Compassionate, the Merciful," he repeated, his voice hoarse but loud enough. "All praise to Allah, Lord of the Worlds," and the rest followed, one stammered letter after the other, one hesitant word after the other.

Silence. The scratch of a pen. His hand in her father's hand. The *Fatiha* again, everyone saying it to themselves, mumbling it fast, raising their palms, "*Ameen*," wiping their faces. "Congratulations, we've given her to you now." "She's all yours now."

When he saw her, when he walked down the corridor to where the women were gathered, when the door opened for him and he saw her, all he could say was, "Oh my God, I can't believe it!" It was as if it were her and not her at the same time – her familiar voice saying his name, those dark slanting eye smiling at him. But her hair long and falling on her shoulders (she had had it chemically relaxed), make-up that made her glow, a secret glamour. Her dress in soft red, sleeveless, she was not thin …

"God, I can't believe it," he said, and the few people around them laughed.

A haze in the room, smoke from the incense they were burning, the perfume making him light-headed, tilting his mind, a dreaminess in the material of her dress, how altered she was, how so much more of her there was. He coughed.

"Is the incense bothering you?" she asked him.

A blur as someone suggested that the two of them sit out on the balcony. It would be cooler there, just for a while, until they could get a lift to the hotel. He followed her out into a sultry darkness, a privacy granted without doors or curtains, the classical African sky dwarfing the city below.

She did not chat like she usually did. He could not stop looking at her and she became shy, overcome. He wanted to tell her she was beautiful, he wanted to tell her about the ceremony, about the last few days and how he had missed her, but the words, any words wouldn't come. He was stilled, choked by a kind of brightness.

At last she said, "Can you see the henna pattern on my palms? It's light enough." He could trace, in the grey light of the stars, delicate leaves and swirls.

"I'll wear gloves," she said, "when we go back to Scotland, I'll wear gloves, so as not to shock everyone."

"No, you needn't do that," he said, "it's lovely."

It was his voice that made her ask. "Are you all right, you're not well?" She put her hand on his cheek, on his forehead. So that was how soft she was, so that was how she smelt, that was her secret. He said without thinking, "It's been rough for me, these past days, please, feel sorry for me."

"I do," she whispered, "I do."

Study Questions

1. How does the description of places in the story enhance the representation of characters and themes?

2. Discuss the plot structure of the story and attempt to identify the exposition, crisis, climax, and denouement.

3. Discuss the significance of the title of the story bearing in mind the main themes and characters. Suggest two other titles you would give to the story.

4. Based on the story's material and your own knowledge from your society, write an essay titled "Traditions, Religion, Love, and Modernity".

Tattoo Marks and Nails

Alex la Guma

The heat in the cell was solid. It was usually hot in the cells, what with over one hundred prisoners packed in, lying on the concrete floor like sardines in a can or tangled like macaroni. But it was the middle of summer, and a weekend when prisoners are locked up early in the day until the following morning, there being only a skeleton staff of guards on duty; it was doubly, perhaps trebly hotter than usual.

The heat was solid. As Ahmed the Turk remarked, you could reach out before your face, grab a handful of heat, fling it at the wall, and it would stick.

The barred windows of the caserne were high up the walls, against the ceiling, and covered by thick wire mesh, its tiny holes themselves clogged and plugged with generations of grime.

We were all awaiting trial. The fact that all such prisoners were deprived of their clothes every time they were locked up in the cells did not make much difference. Naked bodies, or half-naked, only allowed the stench of sweat from close-packed bodies to circulate more freely.

"I know of only one place hotter than this," said Ahmed the Turk, alleged housebreaker, assaulter and stabber. He smiled, flashing his teeth, the colour of ripe corn, in his dark handsome face. "And I don't mean Hell," he added.

Around us were packed a human salad of accused petty – thieves, gangsters, murderers, rapists, burglars, thugs, drunks, brawlers, dope peddlers: most of them by no means strangers to the cells, many of them still young, others already depraved, and several old and abandoned, sucking at the disintegrating, bitter cigarette – end of life.

Now and then pandemonium would reign: different men bawling different songs, others howling or talking at the top of their voices, just for the sake of creating an uproar, others quarrelling violently and often fighting. Here and there parties crouched over games of tattered packs of hand-made or smuggled cards, draughts played with scraps of paper or chips of coal as counters on 'boards' scraped on the floor.

Pandemonium would abdicate for a while when the guard reached the cell door on his rounds around the section and shouted through the peephole in the iron-bound door.

I wiped sweat from my face with a forearm and said: "You were saying something about a place hotter than this."

"Ja," replied Ahmed the Turk. "*Wallahi*. Truly."

"And where would that be?" I asked, "On top of a primus stove?"

"No man," Ahmed replied. "In the Italian prisoner-of-war camp by Wadi Huseni in Libya. I was mos there during the War."

At the other end of the caserne, the Creature, so named after some fantastic and impossible monster of the films, and his gang were persecuting some poor wretch who had arrived that morning. The man, not as smart as others, not able to catch the wire, know the ropes, had been locked up with not even an undershirt on his body. He cringed, stark naked, before the Creature and his henchmen.

The gang leader, and incidentally cell-head by virtue of his brutality and the backing of equally vicious hangers-on, was pointing at the poor joker's bare chest on which something colourfully gaudy had been tattooed, and snarling above the other noises in the cell: "Listen, you *jubas*, there's only one tattoo like that in the whole blerry land. I bet you …"

"What's that basket up to?" I asked.

Ahmed the Turk stuck a crippled cigarette-end between his lips and struck a split match expertly on the wall. "Going to hold a court, I reckon," he said, blowing smoke. "Never liked these prison courts."

A common occurrence in prisons was the 'trial', by the most brutalised inmates, of some unfortunate who might have raised their ire by bootlicking a guard, or rightly or wrongly accused of giving evidence against, squealing on his fellow prisoners, or having annoyed them in some other way. Mock courts, much more dangerous than real ones, were held in the cells and 'sentence' meted out.

There had been the 'case' of a prisoner who had given offence to a cell-boss and his gang. It had been said that he had complained of them to a guard, an unforgivable offence. The gangsters 'tried' him, found him guilty and sentenced him to … he wasn't told. That, as some sadistic refinement, they kept secret among themselves.

The terrified man died a hundred times over before, finally, unable to hold back weariness, he was forced to lie down to sleep. As he lay shivering in some unknown nightmare, a blanket was pressed over his head and face, and a half-dozen knives driven through the one in which he slept.

The next morning the guards found a dead man wrapped in a bloody blanket. No trace of blood on any of the rest of the packed humanity in the cell. There was no sign of a knife. Nobody had a knife, despite searches. The prison inquiry revealed nothing.

"Dammit," I said, taking what was left of the butt from Ahmed. "Hell, that rooker just come in. They got nothing on him."

"Maybe he done something to them outside," the Turk reckoned. He added, "There was a court at Wadi Huseni, too."

"Forget them," he advised, but he was listening to what the Creature was yelling at his gang and the grovelling victim. Then he smiled at me again.

"I was telling you about the P.O.W. camp by Wadi Huseni. Pally, there it was hot. Yellow sand and yellow sky. Man, just sand and sky and some thorn bushes, maybe. And the Sun."

"I was in the Coloured Corps, mos, during the War. Lorry driver. Well some blerry Eyeties supporting the Germans captured us at the time of the Rommel business. So they take us to this camp. A square of barbed wire fence with guards walking round and round it all the time. It was full of our men, Aussies, English and others. And the sun, chommy. Burning, boiling, baking, frying, cooking, roasting."

"The Eyetier lived in tents near the prisoners' camp. We, we had no shelter, nothing man. They fixed up a shelter with sailcloth for the sick and wounded. The rest had to do what they could. Understand?"

Ahmed the Turk grinned. "You call this hot, chommy? Pally, we used to cut slices off the heat, put them on our biscuits and make toast."

I laughed, and wiped some more moisture from my nose. Ahmed the Turk smiled again and scratched himself under his once-gaudy, now grimy and sweat-stained shirt which he had managed to hang onto since he'd come in. He never got out of that shirt.

The Creature was yelling, "... Don't lie, you basket ... We know ... Hear me. I said somebody chopped my brother, Nails, in the back with a knife ... some blerry goose ... Nails' goose, right ... The whore ..."

"The Creature's saying up big likely," Ahmed the Turk said. "His brother, Nails. Just a big mouth like the Creature is, he was. But he had a nice girl, anyway."

"... Couldn't say his name before he died ... But that he had a dragon picked out on his chest, pally ... a dragon, right? ... Maybe like the one you got."

"It wasn't me," the naked prisoners babbled.

"Did you know his brother, Nails?" I asked.

"Yes, man," Ahmed the Turk replied. "Seen him around. Nails, tattoos, courts." He laughed. "Listen, chommy, it reminds me of that court in Wadi Huseni that time."

"Like I was saying, man, it was hot, hot, hot. Water reshun, one tin cup a day. Hot. Hot. Hot."

"After some time, the water supply runs down and the Eyeties are only handing out half a cuppy a day. Man, half a cuppy. Food they could keep. Biscuits and sardines. But water, man, water."

Ahmed the Turk sighed and flicked a rivulet from his brow. The water bucket in the cell itself had just been emptied of the last mouthful and the crowd around it was growling and snapping like mongrels.

The Creature was laughing. It was he who had collared the last of the water, and he was laughing merrily at the others. Then he turned back to his 'prisoner'.

"... Right in the back, hey? ... Nails said we'd know you by that dragon on your chest ... Well, we's got you now, pally ... " He laughed again, the sound coming from his throat like the screeching of a hundred rusty hinges.

"I don't know nothing from it," the man whimpered. "True as God, ou pal."

The creature went on laughing.

"I was telling about the water shortage," Ahmed resumed. "Yes, man. Half-a-cuppy a day in the middle of that seven kinds of Hell."

I said, "You reckoned the tattoo stuff reminded you of something."

"I'm coming to that, man," he said. "Listen. After a while it got so bad everybody was getting pretty desperate for water, hey."

"Then some joker comes up with a scheme. He's got a pack of cards, old, dirty, cracked, but still a full deck. 'Let's play for the water reshun,' this joker say. 'Half-a-cup of water is the limit, and winner takes the lot. Anybody want to play?'"

Ahmed the Turk smiled. "There was helluva lot of *jubas* in that camp wasn't going to take any chances with their water in a card game. Understand? No, pally. They stuck to what they had. But there was some other desperate johns willing to take a chance."

"Further, later on there's quite a clump in the game when the Eyeties have handed out the water. Well, somebody's got to win a card game, don't I say? And one of the boys has a merry old time with nearly two pints of water that he wins."

"Next day the joker with the deck is ready for a game again, quick as the water was handed out. Another rooker wins this time."

"Well, pally, for a couple of days different johns are winning water, and a lot of birds lose their rations. But they are still willing to play."

"Then all of sudden, the luck of the joker who owns the deck changes, and he starts to win the whole pot every day, day after day. Oh, he has a time awright. And with all the losers looking on, likely."

"Dammit, he had water so he could use some of it just to pour over his head like a shower bath, mos. And never parted with a drop of water to the other burgs. There are jokers going crazy for an extra drop in that camp. But our friend just has himself a grand time winning water from a lot of squashies."

"Until the other johns start to think about it."

Ahmed the Turk laughed again and scratched under his shirt. He went on, "Maybe they start reckoning it's funny for

127

this joker to keep on winning all the time. Further, these johns are getting more and more desperate, having no water."

"So, it happens, after the joker had won another game and is pouring his winnings into a big tin he'd got for the purpose, one of the gang, a big Aussie, say, 'Look, cobber. Let's take a look at the deck. Hey?'"

"The joker looks up at the Aussie, while he is pouring cups of water into his tin, and reckons, 'What deck, hey? What about the deck? What for you want to see the deck? The deck's okay, man."

"Let's see the deck, cobber,' the Aussie says. A big boy, like most of those Aussies are. And everybody else is quiet now, looking at the joker, some of them grinning through their beards and their dusty and broken lips."

"'Well, the hell with you,' the joker reckons and starts to get up. The next thing, the Aussie lets go with a fist as big and hard as a brick."

Ahmed the Turk grinned, showing his teeth, and rubbed his jaw, brushing sweat from it and wiping the moist hand on the front of his shirt. At the other end of the caserne, the Creature and his gang were still worrying the naked man, like a pack of dogs with a rat.

"What about the tattoo marks," I asked. I was beginning to eye him with suspicion now.

"I'm coming to that, man," he replied, scowling across to where the Creature and his inquisition were in session. "That pig … Anyway, pally, so this Aussie lets blow with his fist."

"Further, when this joker wakes up, he is flat on his back on the sand with his shirt off, and what's more, he is being held down like that by some of the boys. And looking up, he can see this big Aussie standing over him, smiling and fanning out the deck of cards in his big hands. The joker can't make a move with the men holding him down."

"Then further, the Aussie says: 'Cobber, playing with marked decks, hey! Cheating your pals out of water. hey! Well, cobber, we sort of held a court martial right here, in your—er—absence. Well, cobber, the court has found you guilty, and we're about to carry out the sentence, cobber.' And the Aussie laughs, likely, and everybody else laughs. Except the card joker, naturally. So they carry out the sentence."

"What was it?" I asked.

Ahmed the Turk scowled. 'Why, this Aussie has got a kind of a knife made from a six inch flattened nail. And he uses this to well – not actually – to do some tattooing on the joker's chest – but really some carving.

"Ja, man. They write it on his chest with that long nail, deep into the flesh so it would never go away, while he's struggling and screaming: PRIVATE SO-AND-SO, A CHEAT AND A COWARD. And the joker got to carry those words in scars around with him long as he lives."

I gazed at Ahmed the Turk. Then, "Jesus," I said. "What happened to the joker afterwards?"

Ahmed shrugged. "He escaped. He couldn't stand it, living among those other P.O.W's after that, I reckon. Maybe the basket was collecting that water to get away across the desert, in any case."

"Anyway, soon afterwards, he's gone. Got through the wire somehow, and gone he is." Ahmed the Turk paused. "That's why I said this court of the Creature, and Nails, and Tattooing reminded me also of Wadi Huseni."

"Ahmed," I asked him. "What was the joker's name?"

"I forget now."

He was gazing across the muttering, heaving, writhing tangle of perspiring prisoners to where the gang was holding their 'court'.

"Turk," I said again to him, quietly. "I never did, and nobody here ever did see you with your shirt off, have they?" I was looking at his sweat-stained shirt.

He looked back at me and grinned. "Hell, man. Why should I take it off? Might get pinched. Besides, it isn't as hot here as it was in that Wadi Huseni Camp, mos." He looked again across at the court. "Never did like these prison trials," he muttered. Then shouted, "Creature, you pig! Why don't you leave the poor basket alone? Can't you see he's ... scared?"

The Creature looked across at us, his mob flanking him, the poor naked john grovelling and crying. Then he laughed and, turning away from his victim, began picking a path among the packed prisoners, towards where we squatted. The gang trailed after him, ignoring the naked man. He couldn't get away, could he? The noise in the cell had dropped to an apprehensive mutter.

The Creature made his way across, kicking bodies and legs out of his path, swearing at the impending jumble of humanity.

He was half naked, wearing a pair of filthy pajama pants and, over it, a pair of khaki shorts confiscated from another unfortunate. A ludicrous sight, yet dangerous as a rabid dog. His face was disfigured and reminded one of a tangled knot of rope, with some of the crevices filled in, topped by a blue, badly shaven skull. He came up, sneering with rotten teeth.

Then he stopped, looking at Ahmed the Turk, and laughed.

He said, "Turk, I been sizing you up a long time, mos, Turk. Ou Turk, you reckon, mos, you a hardcase."

Ahmed the Turk laughed at him. The Creature breathed hard into his big chest, and laughed again in return, so that the rope-knot face squirmed and quivered like some hideous jelly.

"Turk," he went on. "Turk, somebody chopped my brother, Nails, in the back. Don't I say! Only thing poor ou Nails knew about the *juba* he had something picked out, tattooed on his chest, man. A dragon, poor ou Nails said."

"Well, Turk, me I been looking for this pig. Don't I say! When I get him; me and my men going to hold court, inside or outside, 'cording to where we get him."

Ahmed the Turk grinned. "What the hell it's got to do with me!" There was a lot of sweat on his face, and he wiped it away, leaving a ditty smear.

The Creature eyed him. "Turk, you been saying up a lot since you come in here … Okay, youse a big, shot, mos … But I been hearing things around, ou Turk. I been hearing things like you was messing around ou Nails' goose, also. Don't I say! Okay. Awright. Maybe it's just talk, hey?"

He laughed again, and then went on. "Okay, Turk, youse a big shot, mos, outside." Then he repeated more or less, my own recent request of Ahmed the Turk. "Come to think about it, Turk. Nobody seen you here with that shirt off, hey? Why don't you take off your shirt, Turk! It's mos hot here, man. Don't I say! Or maybe you heard outside there was word around I was looking for a juba with stuff tattooed on his chest. A dragon, maybe, Turk? Why don't we see you with that shirt off, Turk?"

Ahmed the Turk licked moisture from his lips. He said, "The hell with you."

"Turk," the Creature said. "Turk, my boys can hold you while we pull off the shirt. Just as you like, ou Turk."

The gang edged nearer, surrounding us. Ahmed the Turk looked at the Creature and then looked at me. His face was moist.

Then he laughed, and pulled himself up from his cramped position.

"A wright, all you baskets," he sneered, and unbuttoned his shirt.

Study Questions

1. Describe the atmosphere of the story. Does the atmosphere change as the story develop? Explain.

2. With examples, explain the use of imagery and diction in the story. Discuss their effectiveness.

3. Explain the significance of setting in this story. How does it contribute to and enhance the other elements of the story?

4. Besides imagery and diction, identify and discuss three other literary devices used in the story.

5. With supporting material from the story, write an essay entitled "Crime, punishment and revenge".

Jumping Monkey Hill

Chimamanda Ngozi Adichie

The cabins all had thatch roofs. Names like Baboon Lodge and Porcupine Place were hand-painted beside the wooden doors that led out to cobblestone paths and the windows were left open so that guests woke up to the rustling of the jacaranda leaves and the steady calming crash of the sea's waves. The wicker trays held a selection of fine teas. At mid-morning, discreet black maids made the beds, cleaned the elegant standing bathtubs, vacuumed the carpet and left wild flowers in hand-crafted vases. Ujunwa found it odd that the African Writers' Workshop was held here, at Jumping Monkey Hill. The name itself was incongruous, and the resort had the complacence of the well fed about it, the kind of place where she imagined affluent foreign tourists would dart around taking pictures of lizards and then return home still unaware that there were more black people than red-capped lizards in South Africa. Later, she would learn that Edward Campbell chose the resort; he had spent weekends there when he was a lecturer at the University of Cape Town years ago.

But she didn't know this the afternoon Edward – an old man in a summer hat who smiled to show two front teeth the colour of mildew – picked her up at the airport. He kissed her on both cheeks. He asked if she had had any trouble with her pre-paid ticket in Lagos, if she minded waiting for the Ugandan whose flight would come soon, if she was hungry. He told her that his wife, Isabel, had already picked up most of the other workshop participants and that their friends, Simon and Hermione, who had come with them from London as paid staff, were arranging a welcome lunch back at the resort. They sat down. He balanced the sign with the Ugandan's name on his shoulder and told her how humid Cape Town was at this time of the year, how pleased he was about the workshop arrangements. He lengthened his words. His accent was what the British called "posh", the kind some rich Nigerians tried to mimic and ended up sounding unintentionally funny. Ujunwa wondered if he was the one who had selected her for the workshop. Probably not; it was the British Council that had made the call for entries and then selected the best.

Edward had moved a little and sat closer to her. He was asking what she did back home in Nigeria. Ujunwa faked a wide yawn and hoped he would stop talking. He repeated his question and asked whether she had taken leave from her job to attend the workshop. He was watching her intently. He could be anything from sixty-five to ninety. She could not tell his age from his face; it was pleasant but unformed, as though God, having created him, had slapped him flat against a wall and smeared his features all over his face. She smiled vaguely and said that she had just lost her job before she left—a job in banking—and so there had been no need to take leave. She yawned again. He seemed keen to know more and she did not want to say more and so when she looked up and saw the Ugandan walking towards them, she was very relieved.

The Ugandan looked sleepy. He was square-faced and dark-skinned with uncombed hair that had tightened into kinky balls. He bowed as he shook Edward's hand with both of his and then turned and mumbled a hello to Ujunwa. He sat in the front seat of the Renault. The drive to the resort was long, on roads haphazardly chiselled into steep hills, and Ujunwa worried that Edward was too old to drive so fast. She held her breath until they arrived at the cluster of thatch roofs and manicured paths. A smiling blonde woman showed her to her cabin, Zebra Lair, which had a four-poster bed and linen that smelled of lavender. Ujunwa sat on the bed for a moment and then got up to unpack, looking out of the window from time to time to search the canopy of trees for lurking monkeys.

There were none, unfortunately, Edward told the participants during lunch under pink umbrellas on the terrace, their tables pushed close to the railings so that they could look down at the turquoise sea. He pointed at each person and did the introductions. The white South African woman was from Durban, while the black man came from Johannesburg. The Tanzanian man came from Dar es Salaam, the Ugandan man from Kampala, the Zimbabwean woman from Harare, the Kenyan man from Nairobi, and the Senegalese woman, the youngest at twenty-three, had flown in from Paris, where she was at university.

Edward introduced Ujunwa last, "Ujunwa Ogundu is our Nigerian participant and she lives in Lagos." Ujunwa looked around the table and wondered with whom she would get along. The Senegalese woman looked most promising, with the irreverent sparkle in her eyes and the Francophone accent and the streaks of silver in her fat dreadlocks. The Zimbabwean woman had longer, thinner dreadlocks and the cowries in them clinked as she moved her head from side to side. She seemed hyper, over-active, and Ujunwa thought she might like her, but only the way she liked alcohol — in small amounts. The Kenyan and Tanzanian men looked ordinary, almost indistinguishable – tall men with wide foreheads, wearing tattered beards and short-sleeved patterned shirts. She thought she would like them in the uninvested way that one likes non-threatening people. She wasn't sure about the South Africans — the white woman had a too-earnest face, humourless and free of make-up, and the black man looked patiently pious, like a Jehovah's Witness who went from door to door and smiled when each was shut in his face. As for the Ugandan, Ujunwa had disliked him from the airport, and did so even more now because of his toady answers to Edward's questions, the way he leaned forward to speak only to Edward and ignored the other participants. They, in turn, said little to him. They all knew he was the winner of the last Lipton African Writers' Prize with a prize of fifteen thousand pounds. They didn't include him in the polite talk about their flights.

After they ate the creamy chicken prettied with herbs, after they drank the sparkling water in glossy bottles, Edward stood up to give the welcome address. He squinted as he spoke and the thin hair scattered over his scalp fluttered in the breeze that smelled of the sea. He started by telling them what they already knew—that the workshop would be for two weeks, that it was his idea but of course funded graciously by the Chamberlain Arts Foundation, just as the Lipton African Writers' Prize had been his idea and funded also by the good people at the Chamberlain Foundation, that they were all expected to produce one story for possible publication in the *Oratory*, that laptops would be provided in the cabins, that they would write during the first week and review each participant's work during the second week, and that the Ugandan would be workshop leader. Then he talked about himself, how African literature had been his cause for forty years, a life-long passion that started at Oxford. He glanced often at the Ugandan. The Ugandan nodded eagerly to acknowledge each glance. Finally Edward introduced his wife, Isabel, although they had all met her. He told them she was an animal rights activist, an old Africa hand who had spent her teenage years in Botswana. He looked proud when she stood up, as if her tall and lean gracefulness made up for what he lacked in appearance. Her hair was a muted red, cut so that wisps framed her face. She patted it as she said, "Edward, really, an introduction." Ujunwa imagined, though, that Isabel had wanted that introduction, that perhaps she had even reminded Edward of it, saying, "Now, dear, remember to introduce me properly at lunch." Her tone would be delicate.

Next day at breakfast, Isabel used just such a tone as she sat next to Ujunwa and said that surely, with that exquisite bone structure, Ujunwa had to come from a Nigerian royal stock. The first thing that came to Ujunwa's mind was to ask if Isabel ever needed royal blood to explain the good looks of friends back in London. She did not ask that but instead said—because she could not resist—that she was indeed a princess and came from an ancient lineage and that one of her forebears had captured a Portuguese trader in the seventeenth century and kept him, pampered and oiled, in a royal cage. She stopped to sip her cranberry juice and smile into her glass. Isabel said, brightly, that she could always spot royal blood and she hoped Ujunwa would support her antipoaching campaign and it was just horrible, horrible, how many endangered apes people were killing and they didn't even eat them, never mind all that talk about bush meat, they just used the private parts for charms.

After breakfast, Ujunwa called her mother and told her about the resort and about Isabel and was pleased when her mother chuckled. She hung up and sat in front of her laptop and thought about how long it had been since her mother really laughed. She sat there for a long time, moving the mouse from side to side, trying to decide whether to name her character something common, like Chioma or something exotic, like Ibari.

Chioma lives with her mother in Lagos. She has a degree in Economics from Nsukka, has recently finished her National Youth Service and every Thursday she buys the Guardian and scours the employment section and sends out her CV in brown manila envelopes. She hears nothing for weeks. Finally, she gets a phone call inviting her to an interview. After the first few questions, the man says he will hire her and then walks across and stands behind her and reaches over her shoulders to squeeze her breasts. She hisses, "Stupid man! You cannot respect yourself!" and leaves. Weeks of silence follow. She helps out at her mother's boutique. She sends out more envelopes. At the next interview, the woman tells her she wants somebody foreign-educated, speaking in the fakest, silliest accent Chioma has ever heard and Chioma almost laughs as she leaves. More weeks of silence. Chioma has not seen her father in months but she decides to go to his new office in Ikoyi to ask if he can help her find a job. Their meeting is tense. "Why have you not come since, eh?" he asks, pretending to be angry, because she knows it is easier for him to be angry, it is easier to be angry with people after you have hurt them. He makes some calls. He gives her a thin roll of 200-naira notes. He does not ask about her mother. She notices that the Yellow Woman's photo is on his desk. Her mother had described her well: "She is very fair, she looks mixed, and the thing is that she is not even pretty, she has a face like an over-ripe yellow pawpaw."

The chandeliers in the main dining room of Jumping Monkey Hill hung low that Ujunwa could extend her hand and touch them. Edward sat at one end of the long, white-covered table, Isabel at the other, and the participants in between. The hardwood floors thumped noisily as waiters walked around and handed out menus. Ostrich medallions. Smoked salmon. Chicken in orange sauce. Edward urged everyone to eat the ostrich. It was simply *mah-ve-lous*. Ujunwa did not like the idea of eating an ostrich, did not even know that people ate ostriches, and when she said so, Edward laughed good-naturedly and said that of course ostrich was an African staple. Everyone else ordered the ostrich, and when Ujunwa's chicken, too cirtrusy, came, she wondered if perhaps she should have had the ostrich. It looked like beef, anyway. She drank more alcohol than she had ever drunk in her life, two glasses of wine, and she felt mellowed and chatted with the Senegalese about the best ways to care for natural black hair. She heard snatches as Edward talked about wine: Chardonnay was horribly boring.

Afterwards, the participants gathered in the gazebo, except for the Ugandan, who sat away with Edward and Isabel. They slapped at flying insects and drank wine and laughed and teased one another. You Kenyans are too submissive! You Nigerians are too aggressive! You Tanzanians have no fashion sense! You Senegalese are too brainwashed by the French! They talked about the war in Sudan, about the decline of the African Writers Series, about books and writers. They agreed that Dambudzo Marechera was astonishing, that Alan Paton was patronising, that Isak Dinesen was unforgivable. The Kenyan put on a generic European accent and, between drags at his cigarette, recited what Isak Dinesen had said about all Kikuyu children becoming mentally retarded at the age of nine. They laughed. The Zimbabwean said Achebe was boring and did nothing with style and the Kenyan said that was a sacrilege and snatched at the Zimbabwean's wine glass, until she recanted, laughing, saying of course Achebe was sublime. The Senegalese said she nearly vomited when a professor at the Sorbonne told her that Conrad was really on *her side*, as if she could not decide for herself who was on her side. Ujunwa began to jump up and down, babbling nonsense to mimic Conrad's Africans, feeling the sweet lightness of wine in her head. The Zimbabwean laughed and staggered and fell into the water fountain and climbed out spluttering, her dreadlocks wet, saying she had felt some fish wiggling around in there. The Kenyan said he would use that for his story—fish in the fancy resort fountain—since he really had no idea what he was going to write about. The Senegalese said her story was really *her* story, about how she mourned her girlfriend and how her grieving had emboldened her to come out to her parents although they now treated her being a lesbian as a mild joke and continued to speak of the families of suitable young men. The black South African looked alarmed when he heard 'lesbian'. He got up and walked away. The Kenyan said the black South African reminded him of his father, who attended a Holy Spirit Revival church and didn't

139

speak to anybody on the street. The Zimbabwean, Tanzanian, white South African, Senegalese all spoke about their fathers.

They looked at Ujunwa and she realised that she was the only one who had said nothing and, for a moment, the wine no longer fogged her mind. She shrugged and mumbled that there was really little to say about her father. He was a normal person. "Is he in your life?" the Senegalese asked, with the soft tone that meant she assumed he was not, and for the first time her Francophone accent irritated Ujunwa. "He is in my life," Ujunwa said with a quiet force. "He was the one who bought me books when I was a child and the one who read my early poems and stories." She paused, and everyone was looking at her and she added, "He did something that surprised me. It hurt me, too, but mostly it surprised me." The Senegalese looked as if she wanted to ask more, but changed her mind and said she wanted more wine. "Are you writing about your father?" the Kenyan asked and Ujunwa answered with an emphatic *NO*, because she had never believed in fiction as therapy. The Tanzanian told her that all fiction was therapy, some sort of therapy, no matter what anybody said.

That evening, Ujunwa tried to write, but her eyeballs were swimming and her head was aching and so she went to bed. After breakfast, she sat before the laptop and cradled a cup of tea.

Chioma gets a call from Merchant Trust Bank, one of the places her father contacted. He knows the chairman of the board. She is hopeful; all the bank people she knows drive nice new Jettas and have nice flats in Gbgada. The deputy manager interviews her. He is dark and good-looking and his glasses have elegant designer logo on the frames and, as he speaks to her, she desperately wishes he would notice her. He doesn't. He tells her that they would like to hire her to do marketing, which will mean going out and bringing in new accounts. She will be working with Yinka. If she can bring in ten million naira during her trial period, she will be guaranteed a permanent position. She nods as he speaks. She is used to men's attention and is sulky that he does not look at her as a man looks at a woman and she does not quite understand what he means by going out to get new accounts until she starts the job two weeks later. A uniformed driver takes her and Yinka in an air-conditioned official jeep—she runs her hand over the smooth leather seat, breathes in the crisp air, is reluctant to climb out—to the home of an Alhaji in Victoria Island. The Alhaji is avuncular and expansive with his smile, his hand gestures, his laughter. Yinka has already come to see him a few times before and he hugs her and says something that makes her laugh. He looks at Chioma. "This one is too fine," he says. A steward serves frosted glasses of chapman. The Alhaji speaks to Yinka but glances often at Chioma. Then he asks Yinka to come closer and explain the high-interest savings accounts to him, and then he asks her to sit on his lap and doesn't she think he's strong enough to carry her? Yinka says of course he is and sits on his lap, smiling a steady smile. Yinka is small and fair; she reminds Chioma of the Yellow Woman.

What Chioma knows of the Yellow Woman is what her mother told her. One slow afternoon, the Yellow Woman had walked into her mother's boutique on Adeniran Ogunsanya Street. Her mother knew who the Yellow Woman was, knew the relationship with her husband had been on for a year, knew that he had paid for the Yellow Woman's Honda Accord and flat in Ilupeju. But what drove her mother crazy was the insult of this: the Yellow Woman coming to her boutique, looking at her shoes and planning to pay for them with money that belonged to her husband. So her mother yanked at the Yellow Woman's weave-on that hung to her back and screamed, "Husband snatcher!" and the salesgirls joined in, slapping and beating the Yellow Woman until she ran out to her car. When Chioma's father heard of it, he shouted at her mother and said she had acted like one of those wild women from the street, had disgraced him, herself and an innocent woman for nothing. Then he left the house. Chioma came back from National Youth Service and noticed her father's wardrobe was empty. Aunty Chika, Aunty Rose, Aunty Uche had all come and said to her mother, "We are prepared to go with you and beg him to come back home or we will go and beg on your behalf." Chioma's mother said, "Never, not in this world. I am not going to beg him. It is enough." Aunty Funmi came and said the Yellow Woman had tied him up with native medicine and she knew a good *babalawo* who could untie him. Chioma's mother said, "No, I am not going." Her boutique was failing because Chioma's father had always helped her import shoes from Dubai and Italy. So she lowered prices, advertised in *Joy* and *City People,* and started stocking good-quality shoes made in Aba. Chioma is wearing a pair of those shoes the morning she sits in the Alhaji's sitting room and watches Yinka perch on the expansive lap, talking about the benefits of a savings account with Merchant Trust Bank.

At first, Ujunwa tried not to notice that Edward often stared at her breasts. The workshop days had taken on a routine of breakfast at eight and lunch at one and dinner at six in the grand dining room. On the sixth day, Edward handed out copies of the first story to be discussed, written by the Zimbabwean. The participants were all seated on the terrace and after he handed out the papers, Ujunwa noticed that all the seats under the umbrellas were occupied. It was hot and sunny.

"I don't mind sitting in the sun," she said. "Would you like me to stand up for you, Edward?"

"I'd rather like you to lie down for me," he said. The moment was humid, thick, a bird cawed from far away. Edward was grinning. The others down the table had not heard him. Then the Ugandan laughed. And Ujunwa laughed because it was funny and witty, she told herself, when you really thought about it. After lunch, she took a walk with the Zimbabwean and as they stopped to pick shells by the sea, Ujunwa wanted to tell her what Edward said. But the Zimbabwean seemed distracted, less chatty than usual; she was probably anxious about her story. Ujunwa read it that evening. She thought the writing had too many flourishes, but she liked the story and wrote appreciations and careful suggestions in the margins. It was familiar and funny, about a Harare secondary school teacher whose Pentecostal minister tells him that he and his wife will not have a child until they get a confession from the witches who have tied up his wife's womb. They become convinced that the witches are their next-door neighbours and every morning they pray loudly, throwing verbal Holy-Ghost bombs across the fence.

There was a short silence around the dining table after the Zimbabwean read an excerpt the next day. The Ugandan spoke finally and said there was much energy in the prose. The white South African nodded enthusiastically. The Kenyan disagreed. Some of the sentences tried so hard to be literary that they didn't make sense, he said, and read one such sentence. The Tanzanian man said a story had to be looked at as a whole and not parts. Yes, the Kenyan agreed, but each part had to make sense in order to form a whole that made sense. Then Edward spoke. The writing was certainly ambitious but the story itself begged the question "So what?" There was something terribly passé about it when one considered all the other things happening in Zimbabwe under the horrible Mugabe. Ujunwa stared at Edward. What did he mean by 'passé'? How could a story so familiar be passé? But she did not ask what Edward meant and

143

the Kenyan did not ask and the Ugandan did not ask and all the Zimbabwean did was shove her dreadlocks away from her face, cowries clinking. Everyone else remained silent. Soon, they all began to yawn and say goodnight and walk to their cabins.

The next day, they did not talk about the previous evening. Edward sat at the middle of the table. They talked about how fluffy the scrambled eggs were and how eerie the jacaranda leaves that rustled against their windows at night were. After dinner, the Senegalese read from her story. It was a windy night and they shut the windows to keep out the sound of the whirling trees. The smoke from Edward's pipe hung over the room. The Senegalese read two pages of a funeral scene, stopping often to sip some water, her accent thickening as she became more emotional, each *t* sounding like a *z*. Afterwards, everyone turned to Edward, even the Ugandan, who seemed to have forgotten that he was workshop leader. Edward chewed at his pipe thoughtfully before he said that homosexual stories of this sort weren't reflective of Africa, really.

"Which Africa?" Ujunwa blurted out.

The black South African shifted on his seat. Edward chewed further at his pipe. Then he looked at Ujunwa in the way one would look at a child who refused to keep still in church and said that he wasn't speaking as an Oxford-trained Africanist, but as one who was keen on the real Africa and not the imposing of Western ideas on African venues. The Zimbabwean and Tanzanian and white South African began to shake their heads as Edward was speaking.

"This may indeed be the year 2000, but how African is it for a person to tell her family that she is homosexual?" Edward asked.

The Senegalese burst out in incomprehensible French and then, a minute of fluid speech later, said, "I am Senegalese! I am Senegalese!" Edward responded in equally swift French and then said in English, with a soft smile, "I think she had too much of that excellent Bordeaux," and some of the participants chuckled.

Ujunwa was first to leave. She was close to her cabin when she heard somebody call her and she stopped. It was the Kenyan. The Zimbabwean and the white South African were with him. "Let's go to the bar," the Kenyan said. She wondered where the Senegalese was. In the bar, she drank a glass of wine and listened to them talk about how the other guests at Jumping Monkey Hill—all of whom were white—looked at the participants suspiciously. The Kenyan said a youngish couple had stopped and stepped back a little as he approached them on the path the day before. The white South African said they were suspicious of her, too, perhaps because she wore only kente-print caftans. Sitting there, staring into the black night, listening to drink-softened voices around her, Ujunwa felt a self-loathing burst open in the bottom of her stomach. She should not have laughed when Edward said, "I'd rather like you to lie down for me." It had not been funny. It had not been funny at all. She had hated it, hated the grin on his face and the glimpse of greenish teeth and the way he always looked at her chest rather than at her face, the way his eyes climbed all over her, and yet she had made herself laugh like a deranged hyena. She placed down her half-finished glass of wine and said, "Edward is always looking at my breasts." The Kenyan and white South African and Zimbabwean stared at her. Ujunwa repeated, "Edward is always looking at my body." The Kenyan said it was clear from the first day that the man would be climbing on top of that flat stick of a wife and wishing it were Ujunwa; the Zimbabwean said Edward's eyes were always leering when he looked at Ujunwa; the white South African said Edward would never look at a white woman like that because what he felt for Ujunwa was a fancy without respect.

"You all noticed?" Ujunwa asked them. "You all noticed?" She felt strangely betrayed. She got up and went to her cabin.

She called her mother but the metallic voice kept saying, "The number you are calling is not available at the moment, please try later," and so she hung up. She could not write. She lay in bed and stayed awake for so long that when she finally fell asleep it was dawn.

It was the Tanzanian's turn the following evening. His story was about the killings in Congo, from a militiaman's point of view, a man full of prurient violence. Edward said it would be the lead story in the *Oratory,* that it was urgent and relevant, that it brought news. Ujunwa thought it read like a piece from *The Economist* with cartoon characters painted in. But she didn't say that. She went back to her cabin and, although she had a stomach ache, she turned on her laptop.

As Chioma sits and stares at Yinka's smiling face, she feels as if she is acting a play. She wrote plays in secondary school. Her class staged one during the school's anniversary celebration and, at the end, there was a standing ovation and the principal said, "Chioma is our future star!" Her father was there, sitting next to her mother, clapping and smiling. But when she said she wanted to study literature in university, he told her it was not viable. His word, 'viable'. He said she had to study something else and could always write by the side. The Alhaji is lightly rubbing Yinka's arm and saying, "But you know Savanna Union Bank has better rates, they sent people to me last week." Yinka is still smiling and Chioma wonders whether her cheeks are aching. She thinks about the stories in a metal box under her bed. Her father read them all and sometimes he wrote things on the margins: *Excellent! Cliché! Very good! Unclear!* It was he who had bought her novels; her mother thought all she needed were her textbooks.

Yinka says, "Chioma!" and she looks up. The Alhaji is talking to her. He looks almost shy and his eyes do not meet hers. There is a tentativeness towards her that he does not show towards Yinka. "I am saying you are too fine. Why is it that a Big Man has not married you?" Chioma smiles and says nothing. The Alhaji says, "I have agreed that I will do business with Merchant Trust but you will be my personal contact," he said. Chioma smiles, uncertain what to say. "Of course," Yinka says. "She will be your contact. We will take care of you. Ah, thank you sir!"

The Alhaji gets up and says, "Come, come, I have some nice perfumes from my last trip to London. Let me give you something to take home." He starts to walk inside and then turns. "Come, come, you two." Yinka follows. Chioma gets up. The Alhaji turns again to glance at her, to wait for her to follow. But she does not follow. She turns to the door and opens it and walks out into the sparkling sunlight and past the jeep in which the driver is sitting with the door hanging open, listening to the radio. "Aunty? Aunty, something happen?" he calls. She does not answer. She walks and walks, past the large high gates and keeps walking.

Ujunwa woke up to the crashing sound of the sea, to a nervous clutch in her belly. She did not want to read her story tonight. She did not want to go to breakfast, either, but she went anyway. She said a general good morning with a general smile. She sat next to the Kenyan and he leaned towards her and whispered that Edward had just told the Senegalese that he had dreamed of her naked navel. Naked navel. Ujunwa watched the Senegalese delicately raising her teacup to her lips, sanguine, looking out at the sea. Ujunwa envied her calm. She felt piqued, too, to hear that Edward was making suggestive remarks to someone else and she wondered what her pique meant. Had she come to see his ogling as her due? She was uncomfortable thinking about this, about reading tonight, and so that afternoon, lingering over lunch, she asked the Senegalese what she had said when Edward spoke of her naked navel.

The Senegalese shrugged and said no matter how many dreams the old man had, she would still remain a lesbian and there was no need to say anything to him.

"But why do we say nothing?" Ujunwa asked. She raised her voice and looked at the others. "Why do we always say nothing?"

They looked at each other. The Kenyan told the waiter that the water was getting warm and could he please get some more ice. The Tanzanian asked the waiter where in Malawi he was from. Finally the Zimbabwean said the food at Jumping Monkey Hill was sickening, all that meat and cream. Other words tumbled out and Ujunwa was not sure who said what. Imagine an African gathering with no rice and why should beer be banned at the dinner table just because Edward thought wine was proper and breakfast at eight was too early, never mind that Edward said it was the 'right' time and the smell of his pipe was nauseating and he had to decide which he liked to smoke, anyway, and stop rolling cigarettes halfway through a pipe.

Only the black South African remained silent. He looked bereft, hands clasped in his lap, before he said that Edward was just an old man and meant no harm. Ujunwa shouted to him, "This kind of attitude is why they could kill you and herd you into townships and require passes from you before you could walk on your own land!" Then she stopped herself and apologised. She should not have said that. She did not mean to raise her voice. The black South African shrugged, as if he understood that the devil would always do his work. The Kenyan was watching Ujunwa. He looked both speculative and surprised. He told her, in a low voice, that she was angry about more than just Edward and she looked away and wondered if 'angry' was the right word.

Later, she went to the souvenir shop with the Kenyan and the Senegalese and the Tanzanian tried on jewellery made of faux ivory. They teased the Tanzanian about his interest in jewellery – perhaps *he* was gay, too? He laughed and said his possibilities were limitless. Then he said, more seriously, that Edward was connected and could find them a London agent; there was no need to antagonise the man, no need to close doors to opportunity. He, for one, didn't want to end up at that dull teaching job in Arusha. He was speaking as though to everyone but his eyes were on Ujunwa.

Ujunwa bought a necklace and put it on and liked the look of the white, tooth-shaped pendant against her throat. That evening, Isabel smiled when she saw it. "I wish people would see how faux ivory looks real and leave the animals alone," she said. Ujunwa beamed and said that it was in fact real ivory and wondered whether to add that she had killed the elephant herself during a royal hunt. Isabel looked startled, then pained. Ujunwa fingered the plastic. The cool smoothness was relaxing. She needed to be relaxed, and she said this to herself over and over, as she started to read from her story. Afterward, the Ugandan spoke first, saying how strong a story it was, how believable, his confident tone surprised Ujunwa even more than his words. The Tanzanian said she captured Lagos well, the smells and sounds, and it was incredible how similar Third World cities were. The white South African said she hated that term *Third World,* but she had loved the realistic portrayal of what women were going through in Nigeria. Edward leaned back and said, "It's never quite like that in real life, is it? Women are never victims in that sort of crude way and certainly not in Nigeria. Nigeria has women in high positions. The most powerful cabinet minister is a woman."

The Kenyan cut in and said he liked the story, but didn't believe Chioma would give up the job; she was, after all, a woman with no other choices, so he thought the ending was implausible.

"The whole thing is implausible," Edward said. "This is agenda writing, it isn't a real story of real people."

Inside Ujunwa, something shrank. Edward was still speaking. Of course one had to admire the writing itself, which was quite *mah-ve-lous*. He was watching her, and it was the victory in his eyes that made her stand up and start to laugh. The participants stared at her. She laughed and laughed and they watched her and then she picked up her papers. "A real story of real people?" she said, with her eyes on Edward's face. "The only thing I didn't add is that after I left my coworker and walked out of the Alhaji's house, I got into the jeep and insisted that the driver take me home because I knew it was the last time I would be riding in that it."

There were other things Ujunwa wanted to say but she did not say them. There were tears crowding up in her eyes but she did not let them out. She was looking forward to calling her mother, and as she walked back to her cabin, she wondered whether this ending, in a story, would be considered plausible.

Study Questions

1. Discuss in some detail the setting and the point of view in this story.
2. With reference to any three characters, discuss the strategies the author uses to construct characters in the story.
3. Identify three main themes in the story and discuss their manifestation.
4. What challenges does Ujunwa face as a youth and specifically, as a woman? Relate her experiences to those of youths and women in your society.

5. After returning to Nigeria, Ujunwa attends a convention where she gives a speech. Her speech focuses on the possible solutions to the challenges facing youths and women in her community. Imagine the scenario and write the speech.

Homecoming

Vivienne Ndlovu

He turned the key in the lock, hoping the house might be empty, that Flora would not be there to greet him and he would be given that small space he both wanted and feared. He shut the door firmly behind him, listening for the sounds that would tell him that either Flora or one of the children was at home, but the house was silent. Relief flooded through him, only to be swept away again by the knowledge he needed to face. He carried his travel bag upstairs and into the bedroom he and Flora had shared for the last twelve years. He had returned to it often before, but never like this.

The whole room spoke of Flora, the subtle colours, the simple furnishings – she had never liked fussy things. He would have chosen stronger colours, but this room, though they shared it, was Flora's, he saw now. All evidence of his occupation of it was confined to the cupboards and a copy of '*The Heart of Change*' which lay on the table on his side of the bed. That one small sign of belonging briefly assuaged the dread that had been with him for the last two days, as he sat in meetings, as he went through the motions of getting on the plane, most of all when he had phoned Flora to let her know what time he would be getting in. It had grown in intensity the closer he got to home and now he was here. He had to reach a decision. Flora might return at any moment and he still had no idea what he was going to do.

He had travelled frequently during the early years of their marriage and had taken it for granted that he would seek some woman's company on the trips that took him away the longest. He had given no thought to how Flora would feel about it – men had needs, after all. With equal confidence he assumed

152

that she had always been faithful to him. He had been careful, of course. He generally used protection. But when he had ended up staying in Zambia for almost two years, things got a bit out of hand. Flora had joined him only once, about halfway through his stay, because the children were still young. She had even met Sibongile – the woman had invited them to her home for supper. He hadn't felt even a flicker of guilt at the time.

Since then, he'd travelled a lot less and his lapses had gradually decreased, although he could not claim this was the result of any personal resolve. He remembered the night shortly after his return from Zambia when, after a rather unsatisfactory intimacy, Flora had told him she wanted him to change his work schedule to avoid these long trips away, or perhaps he could find a way for her to travel with him. A few months later still, he had overheard her talking with her sister about the marriage of a mutual friend and been surprised to hear Flora's voice, firm and uncompromising.

"Well I know I wouldn't put up with his carrying on like that. Not now. Not these days."

They had established a good, comfortable marriage and that in itself had dampened his need for other women. It was a couple of years now since he had last gone astray and this was what hit him the hardest. That now, when everything was fine, when he had made the effort to be faithful; when, if he was honest, he had understood the value of having an intelligent and supportive wife (for Flora had surely contributed to the consolidation of his career, with her judicious entertaining and steady urging of his ambition) now, this unwanted news seemed to threaten the whole edifice that was his life. It could all come crashing down around him.

The 'boss' inside his head kept saying he was being ridiculous, their marriage was solid. Good God, this had happened seven years ago. Surely it was just a minor mishap. Something as solid as their relationship would quickly surmount this hurdle and their life together would continue smooth and unblemished, perhaps, be even the richer for it. And anyway, why did he have to tell her? He could try to bury this mistaken, unsolicited knowledge.

Why on earth had he telephoned the woman? He had had only one more day in Lusaka – if only he hadn't made that call. He was at a loose end in the dean's office, waiting for him to come back from a meeting so that they could go out for lunch together when, paging through the paper, he saw an advert for the company she had worked for. Why didn't he just give them a call and see if by chance she was still there. Perhaps if he'd known she was there he wouldn't have done it – perhaps? But the operator answered and put him straight through to Mrs Kamuya and suddenly she was on the other end of the line. She was clearly surprised to hear from him and then he was suggesting a drink that evening and she was agreeing to the invitation. Even then, perhaps he'd assumed she wouldn't be able to make it at such short notice and that she might now have a family of her own … but she had agreed immediately.

By the time she was due to arrive at the hotel, he was looking forward to seeing her. At the back of his mind, he was even anticipating the possibility of sleeping with her again.

He was mildly apprehensive that she might have run to fat, or lost her style in some other way. So it was wonderful to walk into the lobby and see her there, looking almost exactly the same. If anything, maturity had given her even greater appeal, he thought as he approached her. She greeted him with pleasure but refused his suggestion that they go up to his room and instead gestured towards the bar.

"Let's go and have a drink."

They sat, they talked. It was good to see her. He had liked her a great deal. If he hadn't been married, the relationship might have become something more permanent.

Of course she had been married then, too. He hadn't liked to cuckold another man, but Sibongile's husband was a drinker and there had been hints of a violent temper. He had not wanted to know more of her relationship, lest he be somehow drawn in further. But after the waiter had brought her a second drink he thought to ask about the man. She picked up her glass, sipped her drink and setting it down again, "Sam died. Five years ago."

It was a shock, but as he looked at her downcast face, he recognised a new diffidence that made her seem younger, more vulnerable.

"It's been a long time, now," she said, refusing his mumbled apologies. How blithe we are in assuming that those we know and love will continue living and loving as long as we ourselves are alive. And then she had looked him in the eye and said, "He died from TB. It was HIV-related."

As the full realisation of what she was telling him struck home, he was aware of settling his face into an expression of suitable concern and asking her how long he had been ill; and then they were talking about something else, and the moment when he should have asked her about her own status was gone. At the end of the evening, he took down her address and phone number, told her he expected to be back in Lusaka in the coming

155

month and heard himself making the unfounded promise to get in touch then. She had smiled, looking perfectly poised, and said goodbye.

And now, he was here. In this bedroom, this house where his wife lived – the woman he loved, the mother of his children. But who was she? What was her substance when faced with knowledge like this? Flora was, in the end – in argument, in conversation – herself, unfettered by labels like wife, mother, lawyer. Ultimately she judged each situation she faced as who she was at that moment. And with this knowledge, who might she be?

Sam had died so long ago. Was it possible that Sibongile was not infected? His mind refused to deal with the issues. If she was infected, if he was infected, if he had infected Flora … He could die.

He could be responsible for Flora's death. Abruptly he had a mental picture of Flora, ill in bed with a bad flu, just a few months back. It was the first time he had ever seen her succumb to illness and allow herself to be looked after. His heart went cold. Could that have been something more serious? But she was fine now, surely, though maybe she did seem more tired than usual, especially when he had told her about this trip.

He could not fathom how something so far in his past could now return with such vicious power. Everything he believed in, had worked for, it could all be destroyed today, just because of what he knew now. If only he had not called her. How he longed for the felicity of ignorance.

Could he keep silent? Could he quietly go off and have a test? Then, if it was negative, she need never know and their marriage could go on undisturbed. But what if the result was different? He knew he didn't have the courage to face that challenge alone. He needed Flora's strength for that. And he could never go backwards from that, to relive today and then, swollen with deceit and fear, go through the charade of going with Flora for the tests – for of course they would have to go for testing together. And she might still be negative ...

He sat on the bed staring out of the window at the jacaranda tree he and Flora had planted when they had moved into the house. It was just past its full flowering and the tree seemed a foretelling of lost richness, lost abundance. He could not untangle the possibilities the future now thrust upon him and yet he must, for there were Flora's footsteps coming quickly up the path.

Study Questions

1. Explain the main conflict of the story briefly.
2. Describe the character traits of three characters in the story and show how they have been developed?
3. What literary devices are used in the story?
4. The main character resolved to call Sibongile, his former lover, to find out if she had been infected and resolve the doubts in his mind. Imagine this situation and write out the telephone communication.

They Sold My Sister

Leteipa ole Sunkuli

I was only ten years old when my sister was sold away. That was two years ago. A few days before, the suitors had come. Three ugly women and four men. One of the four men wanted to be the husband of my sister. I disliked the way he looked, but my father and the clan liked him very much. They said he came from a rich family. His father had many herds of cattle and a large flock of sheep.

It was true they were rich. They brought as many gifts as I had never seen before. They brought beer; the local busaa and the other type sold in bottles. It was called Libuma. They brought four thick blankets. One for my father, one for my mother, one for my uncle and one for my aunt. Nothing was brought for us children. In fact they did not want children in the house where my sister was sold. I hid myself behind a standing bag of maize. They could not see me. They thought that I was playing with the other children outside. I saw … with my own own eyes. I saw the father of my sister's husband-to-be pull out a wad of red hundred-shilling notes. He gave them to my father. My father's hands quaked as he took the money. My mother smiled. I rubbed my wet eyes. They sold my sister.

One day, much later, my mother beat me up thoroughly when I used the word 'sold', to refer to my sister's marriage. She said 'dowry' was a much kinder and civilised word.

Nyamalo was away in a boarding school. She did not know that at home she had been sold to a man she had seen only once, but never talked with. She did not know that Father and Mother had drunk beer; the beer of the sale. She did not know that Father, Mother, Uncle and Auntie, each had a new

158

thick blanket. She did not know that Father had received, with hands trembling for joy, a fat wad of notes. Cattle would be sent the following day. Nyamalo did not know she was not a member of our household any longer. She was the wife of an ugly man; a man with big eyes and dilated nostrils, like those of a chimpanzee I had seen in a picture. She did not know.

Two days later my father told my brother, Tumuka, to go and bring Nyamalo from school. She had no more reasons to continue schooling when a man had come home for her. After all, which other girls from the neighbourhood attended secondary school? My father used many proverbs to show that it was proper that a Maasai girl of Nyamalo's age should go to her own house. She was already circumcised and her breasts were round enough. My brother, Tumuka, said no. He would not go. Nyamalo was only in her first year of junior secondary school and she must be allowed to finish. "The world has changed," he told Father.

My father's mouth was agape with astonishment. How could a son challenge his father about his own daughter?

"Tumuka!" my father called.

"Yes, papa." Tumuka answered.

"Are you or are you not going?"

"I am not going, papa, and Nyamalo must be let to finish her schooling. She must not be married off at such a tender age. She must be allowed to choose her own man when the time comes." My brother spoke politely but firmly.

"You are not going!" My father retorted. "Alright, you may stay. But Nyamalo will go to her husband whether you like it or not. She is my daughter, not yours. Wait, my dear son, until such a time as you have your own daughter; then you may be listened to. What insolence!"

That was the end of school for Nyamalo. My father brought her home that weekend. The situation was explained to her and I saw a flood of tears run down her sweet cheeks. She screamed, sobbed and writhed painfully on the floor. "I am not going," she said. "I am not going."

My mother also shed a tear. I don't know why Mother shed a tear when she had accepted a blanket, drank beer and smiled when Father was given money.

"You will go, my daughter. You are not your own daughter," Father said resolutely.

"I'm not going," Nyamalo insisted. "What wrong have I done you? Mother! Mother! Why do you forsake me?"

Mother shed more tears and only said between sobs. "It … is … finished …"

Two days later the bride was prepared for the ceremonial departure from her parents' home. She was dressed in a loincloth, a lesso which went under her right arm and was knotted above her left shoulder. A beaded belt went round her waist. Around her neck she wore several strings of beads and one beaded ornament whose bead suspension flowed down to her knees. Her feet were shod in green rubber shoes. On her back she carried a gourd full of milk. A real bride!

The bridegroom's father and mother came to escort her. My father, mother and clan all anointed her with milk cream. They told her to multiply like a pumpkin. May her children fill the world. But they also reminded her that she was now somebody's wife. She must live like one. That would bring great honour not only to herself but to all her people. I was asked to accompany her and to stay with her for two weeks to keep her company.

We walked in a single file. My sister's father-in-law walked ahead, followed by his wife, followed by Nyamalo and, lastly myself. Although customarily the bride was required to promenade along, she defiantly walked clumsily and fast. I heard my father say from behind me when we started off, "This girl will bring us shame."

I could not stay the two weeks I had been asked. I could not stay because of what I saw and heard. After the four days during which the bride stayed with her mother-in-law, we were transferred to the house of Nyamalo's husband. His name, I came to learn, was ole Sirayo. There was no peace between Nyamalo and her husband from the start. She refused to talk to him unless she was asked a question. The first night, instead of going to her husband's bed, Nyamalo came to sleep with me. I felt safe with her sleeping by me, because I was afraid of ole Sirayo. He came to call her. He thought I had slept. I was listening.

"Come to my bed," he said.

"No, I'm not coming," my sister said firmly.

"You are my wife." "No."

"I paid the whole dowry." He grabbed her hand and started pulling her out of bed. "I don't care about dowry. You didn't pay it to me …" She was screaming aloud.

"Don't be stupid! Since when did the Maasai pay bride price to the bride herself?" he went on, towing her away.

"Uuui! Uuui! Uuui!" she screamed at the top of her voice. I also screamed.

"You girl, what are you screaming about?" I did not answer him. My sister went on crying.

"Hey, you in this house, what is happening?" That was the father of my sister's husband. He had come to find out what was happening. "Sirayo!" he called from outside where he stood. "Are you fighting the first night?" "Papa, we are not fighting. It was a small issue."

"What small issue causes all the screaming? Or do you want hyenas to know you are married? Heh! That is not how we treat brides."

My sister's husband kept quiet and his father walked away mumbling something I could not get. As soon as he went ole Sirayo used all his muscle to lift my sister out of bed and carried her to his bed. I covered my head not to see what was happening.

The following morning I told my sister that I must go away. She wept bitterly. She held me to her bosom and let her hot tears flow on to my head. Tears ran down my face. When both of us had no more tears to shed she told me yes, I could go. She said she did not want to see me suffer. I knew she did not want me to see her suffer.

"What are you going to do?" I asked her.

"Learn to love my husband," she said. She led me until we could see our parents' home and she turned back.

Before she left, she embraced me and told me, "Tell Father and Mother that may the wealth they have accepted choke them to death."

I looked into my sister's eyes. I loved my father and mother, but for the first time I wished them dead.

It is now two years since all these happened. And now I fear it is my turn. I am only twelve years old, but I fear. Today I heard something. Ole Timau, the man with a big round stomach and a white beard like one of my father's billy-goat's, came to see my father this morning. They sat on stools in the sitting room and my mother asked me to take tea to them. I served them tea and went to sit under the eaves of the house. I sat near the window that opens into the sitting room. I could hear the two men talk.

"How is everybody in your place?" my father asked.

"They are all fine." Ole Timau answered. "Mm."

"We haven't heard anything offensive to the ear." "Mm."

"Only the ordinary common colds of the nostrils."

"Mm."

"That is the news of the land."

"That is the news of the land," my father tied up the

162

loose end of the traditional Maasai exchange. After the formal exchange of 'news' my father and the man talked about many things. I found the eavesdropping quite interesting. I prayed Mother did not call me to send me somewhere as she was fond of doing. I heard ole Timau tell my father:

"I am soon coming for your heifer."

"A human or animal heifer?"

"Human."

"Which one?"

"There is only one left in your homestead. I speak about the girl, Naliki."

At the mention of my name I froze against the wall.

"For which of your sons will you come?" my father inquired.

"I'll come for myself. I am still young enough to take another wife …"

I did not hear the rest because my mother called me.

"Why are you shivering," she asked me.

"I am afraid." I said in a tremulous voice.

"What of?"

"Nothing." I said.

"Nothing?" "Nothing!" She slapped me. I did not cry.

Now I am afraid. I know soon my father will call for my circumcision. Then I will be sold off like my sister. I will be sold off to an old man with a beard and a big belly. I am afraid. The only person who can save me is Tumuka, my brother. He now works in Nairobi. I must write to him. I must tell him that Father plans to sell me to ole Timau. I am in primary school and I want to finish school. I must be the first Maasai girl to read to the last stage of reading. Tumuka himself told me that. I don't want to marry. But my father will sell me to ole Timau by force.

I will run.

Study Questions

1. What is the story about? Briefly explain in your own words.

2. Describe two of the most emotional episodes in the story.

3. In note form, enumerate the character traits of the main characters and what they represent.

4. How do you respond to the ending of the story? Imagine what transpired afterwards. In four paragraphs write out what likely happened to Naliki and the reactions of the other characters.

Printed in the United States
By Bookmasters